# 24 Hours

That Changed the World

# **24** Hours That Changed the World

## Book

*24 Hours That Changed the World*
Experience the final day in the life of Jesus Christ.
978-0-687-46555-2

## Reflections

*24 Hours That Changed the World: 40 Days of Reflection*
Commit to 40 days of reflection based on Jesus' final day.
978-1-426-70031-6

## DVD with Leader Guide

*24 Hours That Changed the World: Video Journey*
Walk with Adam Hamilton in Jesus' footsteps on the final day.
978-0-687-65970-8

Visit www.AdamHamilton.AbingdonPress.com for more information.

---

### Also by Adam Hamilton

*Enough*

*Seeing Gray in a World of*
  *Black and White*

*Christianity's Family Tree*

*Selling Swimsuits in the Arctic*

*Christianity and World Religions*

*Confronting the Controversies*

*Making Love Last a Lifetime*

*Unleashing the Word*

*Leading Beyond the Walls*

# ADAM HAMILTON

# 24 Hours
## That Changed the World

*Abingdon Press*
*Nashville*

24 HOURS THAT CHANGED THE WORLD

Copyright © 2009 by Abingdon Press.

Scripture quotations in this publication, unless otherwise indicated, are from the New Revised Standard Version of the Bible, copyrighted © 1989 by the Division of Christian Education of the National Council of the Churches of Christ in the United States of America, and are used by permission.

Some Scripture taken from the Holy Bible, TODAY'S NEW INTERNATIONAL VERSION®. Copyright © 2001, 2005 International Bible Society. All rights reserved throughout the world. Used by permission of the International Bible Society.

*This book is printed on acid-free, elemental chlorine-free paper.*

**ISBN 978-0-687-46555-2**

Line illustrations on page 97 by Ken M. Strickland

09 10 11 12 13 14 15 16 17 18—10 9 8 7 6 5 4 3 2 1

MANUFACTURED IN THE UNITED STATES OF AMERICA

To my mom,
Glenda Elizabeth Miller,
whose love and encouragement are a
constant blessing in my life

# Acknowledgments

I AM GRATEFUL to the people of The United Methodist Church of the Resurrection. This book began as a series of sermons shared with this congregation. They are a remarkable congregation, and I am blessed to serve as their senior pastor.

Rob Webster and Alex Schwindt accompanied me to the Holy Land to create the videos that are a companion to this book. Rob Webster provided the editorial work for them. Thanks, Rob and Alex!

Educational Opportunities made possible our trip to Jerusalem to explore this story in the land where the events took place. Special thanks to James Ridgeway.

My assistant, Sue Thompson, has for more than ten years made possible the work that I do. Her work is directly seen in the citations included in the book but indirectly in too many ways to recount.

Special thanks to Rob Simbeck, whose help in editorial revisions and transforming my sermon manuscripts into book chapters was invaluable.

Finally, my partner, wife, and best friend, LaVon Hamilton, has shaped my life and faith. With her I discussed many of the ideas in this book, and she was the inspiration behind the companion volume of daily reflections. My small group was also a great help in shaping the reflections.

*Adam Hamilton*

# Contents

# Introduction

JESUS IS BELIEVED to have died at the age of 33 after a life of approximately 12,000 days. The Gospel writers devoted most of their work to just 1,100 or so of those days, the last 3 years of his life; and their primary interest was in one particular day—the day he was crucified. They believed this 24-hour period changed the world, and each of the Gospels drives toward it.

Beginning Thursday evening after sunset and lasting on through Friday, Jesus would eat the Last Supper with his disciples; pray in the garden of Gethsemane; be betrayed and deserted by his friends; be convicted of blasphemy by the religious authorities; be tried and sentenced for insurrection by Pontius Pilate; be tortured by Roman soldiers; and undergo crucifixion, death, and burial.

When the apostle Paul summarized the gospel for the Corinthian Christians, he did so with these words: "I decided to know nothing among you except Jesus Christ, and him crucified" (1 Corinthians 2:2). The suffering, death, and resurrection of Jesus Christ represent the pinnacle of the gospel and the completion of God's saving work through Jesus.

The aim of this book is to help you better understand the events that occurred during the last twenty-four hours of Jesus' life, see more clearly the theological significance of Christ's suffering and death, and reflect upon the meaning of these events for your life. To do this, we will look at the geographical and historical setting of the events of that fateful day; reflect theologically on Jesus' death; and, ultimately, look to see ourselves in the story, considering how we are like Pilate or Peter, Judas or John.

Our starting point will be Mark's account of the final hours of Jesus' life (Most scholars believe his was the first Gospel written.), but we will supplement Mark's account by looking to the other Gospels.* We will begin with the Last Supper, which took place on Thursday night, and end with Christ's death on the cross the following afternoon. The final chapter will reflect on the Resurrection.

In addition to this book, I have prepared a video that was shot in and around Jerusalem, in the very places where the events described in this book occurred. The video is ideal for use in Sunday school classes, small groups, Bible studies, and book clubs, or for your own personal use. It includes a segment about ten minutes long for each chapter in the book; a printed leader guide is available as well. Many will be interested in studying the last hours of Jesus' life during the Lenten season, and Abingdon Press is also publishing a forty-day reflection guide I have prepared for such persons.

Writing this book and creating the videos on location in Jerusalem have deepened my own faith and my sense of love and gratitude for Jesus Christ. I pray that reading this book will have the same effect on you.

*Adam Hamilton*

---

*Note that the four Gospels differ in numerous details related to the last twenty-four hours of Jesus' life. In addition, interpretations of some of these events differ significantly among scholars. I generally follow Mark's chronology and traditional understandings of these events.

# 24 Hours

## That Changed the World

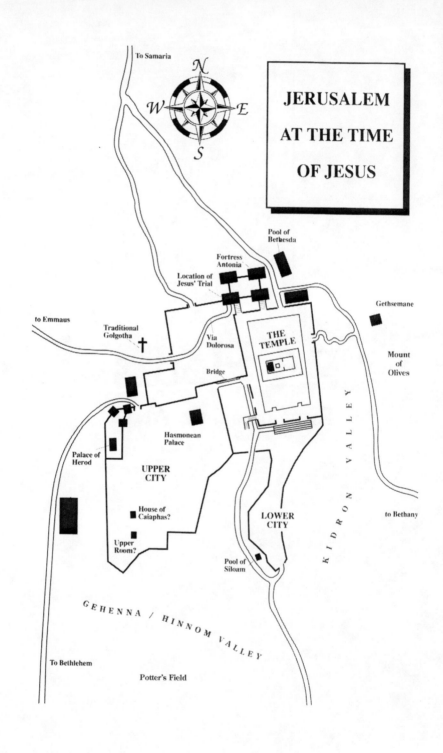

JERUSALEM AT THE TIME OF JESUS

# 1. The Last Supper

*On the first day of Unleavened Bread, when the Passover lamb is sacrificed... he took a loaf of bread, and after blessing it he broke it, gave it to them, and said, "Take; this is my body." Then he took a cup, and after giving thanks he gave it to them, and all of them drank from it. He said to them, "This is my blood of the covenant, which is poured out for many. Truly I tell you, I will never again drink of the fruit of the vine until that day when I drink it new in the kingdom of God." (MARK 14:12, 22-25)*

## Thursday Evening
## AN UPPER ROOM IN JERUSALEM

THE DISCIPLES WERE confused by his words. The Passover Seder was meant to be a time of joy and celebration, retelling the story of God delivering his people from slavery in Egypt. It hinted at the hope that God would send the Messiah. For this reason the meal had special meaning to the disciples; they were convinced that Jesus was the Messiah and that they were in Jerusalem on this Passover so that he could claim his kingdom. Four days earlier the crowds in the city had welcomed him with shouts of

"Hosanna!" Why then was he now speaking of his blood being shed? What did it all mean?

Seldom have the apparent fortunes of any historical figure changed as quickly and dramatically as did those of Jesus in the last week of his life. On Sunday he had entered Jerusalem to crowds strewing palm branches before him, convinced he was the promised Messiah. By Thursday evening he was essentially in hiding, as the city's religious leaders plotted his death with the help of one of the twelve disciples who had been closest to him during his public ministry.

Jesus, of course, knew what was coming. He had foretold all of it, although his disciples never understood. The events of the last twenty-four hours of Jesus' life would test those closest to him, and they would fail.

Jesus had arrived in Jerusalem after walking with his disciples the approximately seventy-five miles from the area around the Sea of Galilee, where he had spent much of his ministry. He had come to celebrate the Feast of Passover, and he had come to die. He entered the city from the Mount of Olives, riding a donkey on which some of his followers had laid their clothing. Throngs of people hailed him, shouting,

> Hosanna to the Son of David!
> Blessed is the one who comes in the name of the Lord!
> Hosanna in the highest heaven! (Matthew 21:9)

In essence they were saying, "Save us now, Jesus. Deliver us."

Jesus looked around the city and then, as evening approached, went back to Bethany, on the Mount of Olives, to stay the night (Mark 11:11).* The next day he made his way to the Temple. There, in the outer court of the Gentiles where all nations were invited to pray, he watched as people bought and sold goods in what amounted to an open marketplace; and he became visibly angry. "Is it not written," he said, " 'My house shall be called a house of prayer for all the nations'? / But you have made it a den of robbers" (Mark 11:17). He overturned the moneychangers' tables and drove out the merchants (Matthew 21:12), infuriating the religious leaders who controlled the Temple.

Jesus returned to the Temple courts each day that week; and as he taught, he pushed harder on his religious reforms, challenging those same religious leaders again and again. "Woe to you, scribes and Pharisees, hypocrites!" he said. "For you are like whitewashed tombs, which on the outside look beautiful, but inside they are full of the bones of the dead and of all kinds of filth" (Matthew 23:27). He chastised them for their spiritual pride, their hard hearts, and their religion of rules that served only to alienate further those who were lost. He told the people, in effect, "Do what the religious leaders tell you to do, but don't do as they do; for they are like the blind leading the blind."

With every charge and challenge, Jesus further angered the scribes, the Pharisees, and the Sadducees. The tension grew each time he entered the Temple. By Thursday, it was clear the city's religious leaders were plotting to put him to death.

## Preparing the Passover Seder

So at noon on Thursday he turned to two of his disciples (Luke tells us it was Peter and John [21:8].) and told them to go into town and prepare for the Passover feast, or Seder, which he and his disciples would eat in private.

Jesus said to his disciples, "Go into the city, and a man carrying a jar of water will meet you, follow him" (Mark 14:13). Carrying water was a woman's job, so such a man would stand out on Jerusalem's busy streets. Some believe Jesus was miraculously able to see what was about to happen, while others believe he had arranged for the meal in advance. In any case, Jesus told the disciples, "Wherever he enters, say to the owner of the house, 'The Teacher asks, Where is my guest room where I may eat the Passover with my disciples?'" (Mark 14:14).

A house like this, by the way, would have been owned by someone who was wealthy. The person was therefore risking wealth, status, perhaps life itself, in order to host Jesus and his disciples.

Everything went just as Jesus had said. Peter and John made the preparations in the upper room—probably the same room where, on the Day of Pentecost, one hundred twenty disciples would gather and find themselves filled with the Holy Spirit, speaking in other tongues. At three o'clock in the afternoon, Peter and John would have taken a lamb to the Temple for sacrifice, joining tens of thousands of people arriving for that purpose throughout the day. As people sang psalms, the lamb's throat would be slit; and a priest would catch the blood in a bowl, then pour it at the base of the altar table. Another priest would butcher the lamb. Peter and John would then take the meat and return to the kitchen at the upper room, where the lamb would be basted in oil or wine and roasted for three or four hours. By about seven o'clock that evening, Jesus and the other disciples would have joined Peter and John in the upper room for the meal.

The Passover Seder they shared is a meal commemorating God's central saving act toward Israel, an event described in Exodus 3–13. The Israelites had been slaves in Egypt for 400 years when God called Moses to deliver them. Moses demanded that Pharaoh release his people, but the Egyptian monarch refused. God then brought a series of plagues upon the Egyptians, but still Pharaoh would not relent. Finally, God said to Moses that he would perform one last terrible deed in the land; after this the pharaoh would have to let the people go. God would strike down the firstborn in every household and among every flock throughout the land of Egypt.

On that night the Israelites were to sacrifice a lamb to God. They were to mark their doorposts with its blood. As the Angel of Death was to pass through the land, it would pass over the homes marked by the blood of a lamb, thus sparing the firstborn in that home. The lamb was to be cooked and eaten, giving the Israelites one final meal, one last supper in Egypt, before they were delivered.

Death did indeed visit the land in the middle of the night, from the humblest dwelling to Pharaoh's palace. In the morning, Egypt was awash in mourning. Amid that devastation, Pharaoh finally relented. He ordered the Israelites to leave Egypt. They prepared to flee so quickly that there was no time to leaven their bread dough and allow it to rise. As a result, the bread they took with them was unleavened.

The Israelites' escape set in motion their epic journey through the wilderness, a forty-year trek that would transform the Israelites into a nation and lead them to the Promised Land. From that day forward, the Israelites annually celebrated the Passover that had accompanied their escape from bondage in Egypt; and the meal would be forever known as the "Feast of Unleavened Bread." Exodus 12 records how God commanded the Israelites to prepare this meal—to sacrifice and roast the lamb and to eat unleavened bread and bitter herbs in memory of their deliverance from slavery to freedom.

"It is a meal filled with ritual," says Rabbi Amy Katz, a friend with whom my wife (LaVon) and I have shared the Passover Seder, "from the food you eat to how you eat it to how you sit." LaVon and I had the joy of joining Rabbi Katz for a wonderful Seder meal that included brisket, chicken, vegetables, and delicious desserts. Interspersed throughout the meal was a discussion of the foods that symbolically retell the story of Israel's deliverance. We ate bitter herbs—horseradish and parsley, reminders of the bitterness the Israelites had experienced when they were slaves in Egypt. The herbs were dipped in salt water, which represented their tears. We ate the charoset, a pureed apple mixture meant to look like the mortar out of which the Israelites made bricks for Pharaoh's building projects. An egg reminded us, as it reminds Christians at Easter, of new birth and new life, that Israel experienced a new beginning. The unleavened matzoh reminded us of the haste of the Israelites' escape. The lamb was a reminder of the lamb slain that original Passover, whose blood marked the doorposts of the Israelites' homes and ensured that death "passed over." Finally, we drank four small cups of wine as a reminder of God's promises that he would redeem the Israelites (See Exodus 6:6-7.).

We began at seven o'clock in the evening, and it was close to midnight before we finished. This was undoubtedly similar to the Seder that Jesus and his disciples ate together. These same items—the wine, the unleavened bread, the bitter herbs—were all placed on the table in that upper room. In that case, though, the good food, the deep friendships, and the story of God's deliverance of Israel from slavery would have been tempered by the heaviness of Jesus' heart. He knew, as his disciples did not, that this was the last time he would share this meal with them.

Reliving the meal with Rabbi Katz helped me understand, among other things, why the disciples, so full of food and wine at such a late hour, fell asleep in the garden of Gethsemane as Jesus prayed and urged them to watch with him.

The meal also prompted me to look even more closely at the Gospel descriptions of the Last Supper. John goes into great detail, providing us with the most complete account of what Jesus said that night. Interestingly, John's account is unique among the Gospels in seeing the Last Supper as a kind of "pre-Passover" Seder. He has Jesus suffering on the cross at the very time when the Passover lambs were being sacrificed (John 19:14)—a powerful image that helps John make a theological point.

Various efforts have been made to harmonize the two differing timelines, and I will let you explore these on your own. John does not have Jesus telling his disciples to "do this in remembrance of me." He does not describe the bread and the wine. Instead, he devotes five chapters to describing what Jesus taught and what he prayed that evening during the meal. Chapters 13 through 17 of John contain some of the most loved verses in the Bible and describe Jesus teaching by example, as when he washed the disciples' feet, showing them that greatness in the kingdom of God is found in serving others. (For further reflection on John's account, see the book of reflections that is a companion to this volume.)

### Betrayal and Repentance: Preparing Ourselves

The Passover is meant to be a festive and celebratory time, filled with joy as participants remember that those who were slaves were now set free, at last becoming one people, the people of God. If indeed the Last Supper began with such a tone, it changed during the course of the evening. Even beyond Jesus' foreknowledge of events, there was great apprehension in the room. Everyone was conscious of the heightened tension between Jesus and the religious leaders. They all wondered what was going to happen to Jesus—and to them. Would there be repercussions from his actions in the Temple? Might he finally proclaim himself as Messiah?

Jesus cut through the uncertainty with a statement so electric it still echoes across the centuries. "One of you," he said, looking at them in the sudden stillness of the Seder celebration, "will betray me" (Mark 14:18).

He knew which one it was, but he did not say. "Surely, not I?" the disciples asked (Mark 14:19). "It is one of the twelve, one who is dipping bread into the bowl with me" (Mark 14:20), Jesus said, probably referring to the bowl of charoset before them.

The story of the betrayal winds its way through the rest of the Gospel accounts of the final twenty-four hours of Jesus' life. Before the night was through, Judas would betray Jesus; Peter would deny him; and the disciples would desert him, leaving Jesus utterly alone as he faced trial at the hands of his enemies.

The echoes of Jesus' prediction and of the acts of betrayal by those closest to him are still discomfiting. In our own age, when church leaders have abused children, embezzled funds, and more, we realize that such betrayals are commonplace. Jesus might well have said, "All of you will betray me"; and with that realization, we must look finally at ourselves.

When have you been Judas? When have you been Peter or the other disciples? When have you betrayed Jesus or denied or deserted him? The reality is that all of us will at some time betray him—every one of us.

Several weeks ago I was greeting worshipers in the narthex of our church building, and I saw a couple who had not been in attendance for quite a while. I went up to greet them and said, "It's so good to see you." The man said to me, "I haven't been here for some time because I did something that I knew disappointed God, and I just couldn't bring myself to come back." That man could be any one of us. All of us will disappoint God. All of us will betray him.

When we commemorate the Last Supper in the act of receiving Communion, we would do well to recall this part of the meal: Jesus' acknowledgement of the betrayal, the denial, the desertions that would follow. I suspect this is why the church has traditionally called for confession and repentance before we receive the bread and wine. In the Communion liturgies of many churches, there is a confession that speaks of having sinned against the Lord "by thought, word and deed . . . by what we have done, and what we have left undone."

An entire season of the Christian liturgical year is devoted to the idea of repentance for our acts of betrayal and desertion. Lent, in the early church, was a time when those who had publicly denied Christ in order to avoid persecution repented and were restored, were brought back into fellowship and allowed to receive Holy Communion again.

It is worth considering, as we look at repentance and restoration, that although Jesus knew Judas would betray him, Peter would deny him, and the others would desert him, he still washed their feet (John 13:3-5), then shared the bread and wine with them—bread that represented his body and wine that represented his blood. Despite knowing what they would do, he said to them, "I do not call you servants any longer... but I have called you friends" (John 15:15). He did that for all of them, including Judas. Jesus looked past their betrayal, their sins, and their failures and called them his friends. We take comfort in the knowledge that he will do that for us as well.

## "This Is My Body..." (Mark 14:12): From Seder to Eucharist

After announcing his betrayal, Jesus took the matzoh and said a blessing over it. But what he said next left his disciples perplexed. As he broke the matzoh and handed it to his disciples, he said, "Take, eat; this is my body" (Matthew 26:26). That was not part of the Haggadah, the text that sets out the order of the Passover Seder. It was, rather, a startling and striking object lesson. Jesus regularly spoke in parables, using analogy, simile, and metaphor. In this case, the bread he held stood for his body, which only a few hours later would be lashed with the stripes of a scourge, then pierced with nails as he hung on a Roman cross. As had happened so often, the disciples did not understand the analogy or what was about to happen. Nonetheless, they ate.

Then Jesus took the cup—likely the third of the four cups of wine the disciples would have drunk at the Seder—and again he left them puzzled when he said, "This is my blood of the covenant, which is poured out for many for the forgiveness of sins" (Matthew 26:28). This reference to the cup of redemption was again not part of the Passover Seder, although the disciples would have recognized the phrase "blood of the covenant." We find it in Exodus 24:8, when, as God enters into a formal relationship with Israel, Moses takes the blood of bulls and sprinkles it on the people, saying, "See the blood of the covenant." Perhaps the disciples remembered that God had spoken again through Jeremiah:

> The days are surely coming, says the LORD, when I will make a new covenant with the house of Israel and the house of Judah. It will not be like the covenant that I made with their ancestors when I took them by the hand to bring them out of the land of Egypt—a covenant that they broke, though I was their husband, says the LORD. But this is the covenant that I will make with the house of Israel after those days, says the LORD: I will put my law within them, and I will write it on their hearts; and I will be their God, and they shall be my people. No longer shall they teach one another, or say to each other, "Know the LORD," for they shall all know me, from the least of them to the greatest, says the LORD; for I will forgive their iniquity, and remember their sin no more.
>
> (Jeremiah 31:31-34)

The Israelites had been bound to God, said God through Jeremiah, as a wife is bound to a husband; but they had cheated, turning away from God on many occasions. And so God said, in effect, "I will have to enter into a new covenant with you." Surely Jesus had these words in mind as he handled the cup; and surely this has become the story not just of the Hebrew people, but of all of us—a story of our brokenness and betrayal and our need for forgiveness.

When Jesus said, "This is my blood of the covenant, which is poured out for many for the forgiveness of sins" (Matthew 26:28), he changed everything. He transformed the Passover Seder, giving to all people instead the Eucharist: Holy Communion. The Israelites had become a covenant people by the blood of animals; the Last Supper was the establishment of the new covenant by the blood of Jesus, not only with the tribes of Israel, but with all humanity. Where the Seder was once the story of God's liberation of the Israelite slaves, it was from this time forward the story of God's liberation of all humankind from slavery to sin and death. In that moment, God gave the entire human race new life and a new beginning and made those who choose to follow Jesus into his people, his bride. In this meal and through his death and resurrection, Jesus invited all humankind to become God's covenant people.

The last twenty-four hours of Jesus' life is the story of God whose love for his people is so amazing and profound that he would send his Son to lay down his life as the sign and seal of a covenant that would deliver the human race from death. God would, by the Spirit, place his commands on their hearts; and he would forgive their iniquity and remember their sins no more.

Paul reminds us in his first epistle to the Corinthians that Jesus said, "Do this...in remembrance of me" (1 Corinthians 11:25). The Last Supper was meant to be repeated in commemoration of the new covenant, just as the Passover Seder was meant to commemorate the central sign of God's saving act in the Hebrew Bible. This meal, this new Passover, the Eucharist or Holy Communion, would be a perpetual reminder of God's love, his grace, and the sacrifice of his Son. It would be the meal by which we as Christians would remember our story. By means of it, our lives would be reshaped.

If we understand Holy Communion to be analogous to the Passover Seder, we would do well to tap into Jewish insight about this ancient ritual meal. Knowing what it means to the Jewish people and how it affects their lives will help us see how Jesus looked at the Seder and the effect he intended Holy Communion to have on us.

"[The Passover Seder] is the time when we remember, as recorded in the Book of Exodus, how we cried out to God when we were slaves and how God heard our cry and took us out of Egypt," says Rabbi Katz. "That's a big story. It's also the defining story of how we were born as a people. The purpose of the Seder is to make this story accessible to everyone at the table in any way we can. They've got to get it, because it is our most important story."

The promise of the Seder, she tells us, is reflected in a line that is traditionally sung during the evening. It comes from the Mishnah; and it says that in every generation, people should see themselves as if they were slaves in Egypt. "You start out as a slave," she adds; "and at the end of the night you are free."

In what way is the Christian Eucharist meant to help Christians recall our own slavery and deliverance?

## A Meal That Defines Us

In transforming the Passover into the Eucharist, I believe Jesus was expecting this meal to define who we are. Through it, we remember that someone saved us; that our freedom came at the cost of a person; that God, walking in human flesh, suffered and died for us. This is the story we remember. It is a big story, and we have to get it if we are going to be a follower of Jesus Christ. We must see ourselves there at that supper and at that cross, knowing it was for each of us that Jesus died. Every time we take the bread and wine, we remember; and it reshapes us. It reminds us where we came from, and it defines who we are and who we will be. It is the remembrance, for Christians, of our birth as a people. We come into that meal remembering that we were slaves to sin and death, living for ourselves and on our own. We leave that meal free, knowing our Savior, choosing to follow him, accepting his grace and mercy in our lives. It is a celebratory event, filled with joy because it represents our salvation. We call it "Eucharist" from the Greek word for thanksgiving. It is a profound and holy meal, filled with good news. That is how it is meant to affect us.

What memories define you? Are there events or words that play over and over inside your head? Is it the abuse you suffered as a child? words spoken by a parent, teacher, or friend? a slight or put-down that still cuts you to the quick? a hurt you cannot let go? a habit, activity, or addiction that controls you?

Those things are not meant to define you. There is something else, a larger story, that defines you. For the Jewish people, that larger story, passed on anew each year, is the memory of the Passover, summed up in the words, "We once were slaves, but now we're free." For you and me as Christians, our defining story is accompanied by a meal and some important words: "On the night when he was betrayed [Jesus] took a loaf of bread, and when he had given thanks, he broke it and said, 'This is my body that is for you. Do this in remembrance of me.' In the same way he took the cup also, after supper, saying, 'This cup is the new covenant in my blood. Do this, as often as you drink it, in remembrance of me.' For as often as you eat this bread and drink the cup, you proclaim the Lord's death until he comes" (1 Corinthians 11:23-26).

Bishop Melito of Sardis, in one of the oldest Christian sermons recorded outside the New Testament, noted that the Passover celebration was meant not only to remind the Israelites of God's saving work through Moses but also to point them *toward* what he would do for the entire world 1,200 years later in Jesus Christ.[1] In the same way, we believe Holy Communion takes us back to the cross to remind us what God has done to save us; but it also points us *ahead* to the day when we will eat this meal in the king-dom of heaven. Paul expressed the same thought when he said we are to eat this meal as a way of proclaiming Christ's death until he comes again (1 Corinthians 11:26).

There is one more thing to remember as we reflect upon the Last Supper: As Jesus approached his death, he found it com-forting to be with his friends. In Luke, we read that Jesus said to his disciples, "I have eagerly desired to eat this Passover with you" (Luke 22:15). In John's account, Jesus told the disciples of his love for them and called them not servants or pupils, but friends (John 15:15). In the hours before Jesus would be arrested, tried, and held for crucifixion, he was with twelve men who were his companions and intimates, men with whom he had prayed, worshiped, and shared life. When he went to pray, know-ing he would die, he asked those who were closest to him to pray with him.

Remember, these close companions were not perfect. They had let him down and would do so again. One would even betray him. Still, they were the best friends he had; and they were with him as he approached his darkest hour.

The earliest Christians gathered for worship in the Temple courts and met in smaller groups in one another's homes, as Jesus had met with his small group. Many modern churches emphasize small groups because, like Jesus, each of us needs close friends who will join us on this journey, who will challenge us, help us, and support us in our faith. This was important for Jesus, and it is important for all of us.

If you knew you had one more day to live, that it was time for your last supper, who would be sitting around your table? No doubt your family members would be there. LaVon and my daughters would be there for me, as would my parents, if they could. The others in that room would be from my small group. They are the people with whom I meet every week to pray and to study the Scriptures. They have encouraged and blessed me again and again over the years. We have visited each other in the hospital. We have prayed for one another through difficult times. We have done life together, and as a result these people have become some of my closest companions.

I am wondering if you have spiritual friends like that, people who will pray you through tough times, people you can talk to about the faith, people you can confess to and who can confess to you—people who carry one another to Jesus.

Jesus needed friends like that. You need them too. I am reminded of a man in the congregation I serve who found such friends in our evening men's study. His cancer returned after being in remission for two-and-a-half years. During the last year-and-a-half of his life, when he could no longer attend that small group, these guys carried him. They prayed for, encouraged, blessed, and loved him to the end. At his funeral they all were there, a band of brothers who had done life together.

When a woman in our congregation was diagnosed with stage three ovarian cancer, her small group began praying for and encouraging her. When she began to lose her hair during treatment, one of the men came to the group one night with his head shaved. He told her, "I'm not going to have any hair until yours comes back." It was his way of saying, "We're walking through this together because I am your brother in Christ." They both celebrated when her hair grew back.

Friendships like that do not just happen. You have to cultivate them. Your local church likely has a small-group ministry. If not, invite some of your acquaintances, neighbors, or friends to join you in starting such a group. Gather weekly for prayer, study, and mutual encouragement. Jesus needed a group like this; and if he did, how much more do we need such a group?

At the Last Supper, Jesus sat with his disciples, a band of misfits and ragamuffins. There were fishermen, a tax collector who was a Roman collaborator, a Zealot who wanted to kill the Romans, a mix of brash and bashful men, most of whom (like most people in the first century) could not read and write. One would betray him, one would deny him, all would desert him; but they were still his friends. In breaking bread with them, he taught them one last time. He showed them his love. In the Gospel of John we read that he washed their feet. He gave them a meal by which they would remember him for the rest of their lives. And from that time to the present, every time Jesus' disciples have shared this meal of bread and wine, it has bound them together as his followers and reminded them that he is never far away.

---

[1]From "On the Passover," by Melito of Sardis; see The Crossroads Initiative, http://www.crossroadsinitiative.com/library_article/817/On_the_Passover_Melito_of_Sardis.html. (March 1, 2006)

*This is true only in the Gospel of Mark (11:11). In Matthew's and Luke's Gospels, Jesus enters the Temple area right away and begins to overturn the moneychangers' tables.

# 2. The Garden of Gethsemane

*They went to a place called Gethsemane. (MARK 14:32a)*

## Thursday Night
### ACROSS THE KIDRON VALLEY

SOMETIME AFTER ELEVEN o'clock on Thursday night, Jesus and his disciples concluded their Passover Seder by singing a hymn. We know the words they sang because this hymn, like the prayer Jesus spoke as he blessed the bread, is still a part of the Seder. It is called the Hallel, a word meaning "praise" (It is the root of our word "hallelujah"), and it is composed of selected verses from Psalm 113 to Psalm 118. It was the Hallel that the people quoted as they cried out four days earlier, "Blessed is the one who comes in the name of the LORD" (Matthew 21:9; see Psalm 118:26). It is also in the Hallel that we read, "The stone that the builders rejected / has become the cornerstone" (Matthew 21:42; see Psalm 118:22), a passage on which Jesus preached during this last week of his life.

I cannot help but wonder if Jesus drew particular comfort from these verses as he and his disciples sang this ancient hymn before walking to the garden of Gethsemane:

> Out of my distress I called on the LORD;
> the LORD answered me and set me in a broad place.
> With the LORD on my side I do not fear.
> What can mortals do to me? . . .
> I shall not die, but I shall live,
> and recount the deeds of the LORD. . . .
> I was pushed hard, so that I was falling,
> but the Lord helped me.
> The LORD is my strength and my might;
> he has become my salvation. (Psalm 118:5-6, 17, 13-14)

I suspect these words continued to echo in Jesus' mind as he prayed that night in the garden. Jesus turned regularly to the psalms, drawing from them throughout his public ministry. He taught from the psalms, he sang from the psalms at the Last Supper, and it was the psalms that he prayed as he hung on the cross. Clearly they were an important part of his spiritual life. If we seek to learn spiritually from Jesus, we will want to become familiar with the psalms. Like Jesus, we will draw comfort from selected verses. The Gospels do not show him reciting entire psalms but rather choosing this or that verse, often drawing on beautiful, noble, and lofty verses nestled among less noble, even vengeful, verses in particular psalms.

The psalms represent the heart and soul of the Bible, and Jesus' use of them during the last twenty-four hours of his life beckons us to become more familiar with them. A good starting point might be to read Psalm 118 in its entirety, imagining what these words may have meant to Jesus as he sang them on that agonizing night.

## "You Will All Become Deserters" (Mark 14:27a)

After leaving the upper room, Jesus led his disciples east and then north on the road that ran along the Kidron Valley. On their right were the tombs of priests, prophets, and ordinary people who were buried there, facing Jerusalem.

The Kidron Valley is also called the Valley of Jehoshaphat, and in Joel 3:12 it is identified as the site of the Last Judgment:

> Let the nations rouse themselves,
>     and come up to the valley of Jehoshaphat;
> for there I will sit to judge.

This valley represents the place where all the nations of the earth will one day be gathered to be judged by the one who, on this tragic night, led his disciples along the dark road. Surely this fact would not have been lost on Jesus.

At the last supper Jesus had predicted that one of the disciples would betray him. Now, as he walked with his friends, Jesus predicted that all of them would desert him. This prediction captures one part of the grief Jesus experienced that night. He knew Judas had already sold him out for thirty pieces of silver and would soon betray him with a kiss. He knew the disciples would all desert him, fleeing to protect their own lives. He knew that Peter, despite his protestations to the contrary, would deny even knowing him. The experience of being betrayed, deserted, and denied by his closest friends—this would produce great sorrow in any man. It was doubly true for Jesus because these were his closest companions, men who had been with him for three years, who saw him work miracles and heard him preach. I am strangely grateful that the Gospel writers included this information rather than glossing over what was surely an embarrassing testimony concerning the disciples. The very fact that they failed the Lord helps me trust that there is grace yet for me when I deny, desert, and betray him.

The comfort I draw from the story is not simply that even those closest to Jesus failed him but that Jesus knew this would happen. Following his prediction that they would fall away, Jesus looked beyond their betrayal and said, "After I am raised up, I will go before you to Galilee" (Mark 14:28). He anticipated their desertion, but he also foretold their restoration. He would take them back despite the fact that they would forsake him; and if he did this for them, he will do this for me and for you.

## The Garden

At the base of the Mount of Olives, overlooking the Kidron Valley, sits a grove of olive trees called the garden of Gethsemane. The garden looks directly onto the east wall of the Temple Mount, upon what is known as the Golden Gate, or the Beautiful Gate (an entrance sealed in 1541 by Sultan Suleiman I). This gate is described in Ezekiel 44 as the place where a "prince" would one day enter the Temple courts. Is it possible that Jesus chose to come here to pray for this very reason?

Today, the garden of Gethsemane includes several very old olive trees. Some suggest these trees date from the time of Jesus; but as with many things in the Holy Land, others dispute this. Regardless, these trees have stood for hundreds of years, reminding pilgrims of the night when Jesus prayed here.

Nearby sits the Church of All Nations, built atop previous churches to commemorate both Jesus' agony in the garden and the site of the Final Judgment. The church takes its name from Joel and his reference to the nations gathering for that momentous event. Entering the church, you can visualize that night when Jesus and his disciples came to the garden to pray. The church is darkened. Stars dot the ceiling. At the chancel, a short iron fence surrounds a large stone outcropping. Tradition holds that this is the very place Jesus prayed that night as he awaited his arrest. Modern pilgrims can kneel to pray around the rock and can even touch it. It is a moving experience meant to take the worshiper back to that first Maundy Thursday.

To the north of the ancient trees and the Church of All Nations is a grove of younger olive trees. It is seldom visited, but it gives perhaps a better sense of what the garden may have looked like when Jesus and his disciples came to pray. Somewhere in the grove was an olive oil press, for this is the meaning of the word *Gethsemane*.

John alone tells us that the place Jesus prayed was a "garden" (John 18:1). He alone also tells us that the tomb where Jesus was buried was in a garden (John 19:41) and that when Mary Magdalene first saw the risen Christ, she thought he was a gardener (John 20:15). Perhaps John intends us to make the connection between what Jesus was doing and the events that took place in another garden, at the very beginning of the Bible. God was the gardener who planted the garden called Eden. And it was in that garden that Adam and Eve disobeyed God and Paradise was lost. John wants us to recognize that Jesus, unlike Adam, would be faithful to God. John also wants us to see that what Jesus was about to do was intended to address, and reverse, the effects of Adam and Eve's "fall." In fact, Paul went so far as to speak of Jesus as the "last Adam" (1 Corinthians 15:45).

## "Sit Here While I Pray" (Mark 14:32): The Anguish of Jesus

John tells us Judas knew where to find Jesus on this night "because Jesus often met there with his disciples" (John 18:2). Luke writes that Jesus went to the Mount of Olives to pray that night, "as was his custom" (Luke 22:39). Why, we might ask, did

Jesus often go to this place? Was it the beauty of the grove? Was it the fact that from this vantage point he could see the Temple Mount? Was it because David had gone up the Mount of Olives near this place, weeping after he was betrayed by his son Absalom and his servant Ahithophel? Was it perhaps a way of connecting with the words of Zechariah the prophet concerning the Messiah: "On that day his feet shall stand on the Mount of Olives" (Zechariah 14:4)? Or was this simply a peaceful and serene place where he felt particularly close to God? It was likely for all these reasons. What we know for certain is that Jesus had regularly come to this place to pray, and it was to this place to which he returned when he was in his greatest anguish.

As they entered Gethsemane, Jesus asked his disciples to watch and pray. Then he took Peter, James, and John with him a bit farther into the garden. He did not speak of or display his anguish until he was alone with his three closest companions. It is possible that he felt the need to be strong for the others and to keep them from seeing his torment, while still needing to share it with someone. Perhaps he felt these three might be able to understand.

Most of us know how difficult it is to be strong for others; yet we are hesitant to reveal those moments when we are afraid, angry, or grieving. Still, we all need close companions with whom we can share such feelings. We need our Peter, James, and John. Often, like Jesus with his companions, we do not need our friends to say anything in our times of sorrow. Jesus did not ask Peter, James, and John for advice, or even for words of encouragement. Like us, he just wanted to know they were there.

Finally, Jesus began to reveal what he was feeling. Matthew tells us he "began to be grieved and agitated" (Matthew 26:37). Jesus told them, "I am deeply grieved, even to death; remain here, and stay awake with me" (Matthew 26:38). He then went a few paces farther and "threw himself on the ground" to pray

(Matthew 26:39). After a short time, he came back to his friends. Did Jesus need to talk with them or simply to know they were with him? We do not know. We do know he found them sleeping, and his disappointment was clear. He asked Peter, "So, could you not stay awake with me one hour?" (Matthew 26:40). It was in this context that Jesus spoke those famous words that serve perhaps not so much as a warning, but as a note of grace to his friends: "The spirit indeed is willing, but the flesh is weak" (Matthew 26:41). Here I find myself again identifying with the disciples. This part of the story is powerful precisely because we all can imagine ourselves after midnight, falling asleep when Jesus needs us to be awake and in prayer. Besides offering us grace, this small detail increases the sense that Jesus would drink from the cup of suffering alone.

The idea that Jesus was in anguish, pleading with God, is unsettling to many Christians. For some, the scene evokes great compassion. For others, the image of Jesus asking God to take the cup of suffering from him and his apparent anxiety over the Crucifixion seems to lack nobility and courage. For still others, the image may even appear to indicate a lack of faith. They would perhaps expect Jesus to face his torture and death without agitation or fear. Interestingly, Luke reduces this story by half and seems to minimize Jesus' anguish (though a later editor seems to have added to Luke's Gospel the detail that Jesus' sweat was like drops of blood [Luke 22:44], as though attempting to address Luke's minimalist approach). John does not include the story of Jesus' anguish at all.

Some Christians, in explaining Jesus' agitation and sorrow and his later "cry of dereliction" from the cross ("My God, my God, why have you forsaken me?" [Mark 15:34]), suggest it was not the result of fear or a lack of confidence in the plans of God or even of a desire to avoid torture and death. Instead, their view of Gethsemane and Jesus' recitation of Psalm 22:1 from the cross reflects a particular view of the doctrine of the Atonement. They suggest that when Jesus was hanging on the cross, God placed on him the sins of the world. At that moment, they teach, God turned his face away from Jesus and there was for the first time a separation of the Father from the Son. It is said that this "turning away" was necessary because God is holy and could not look upon the sins of the world when they were placed upon his Son. According to this view, it was this "turning away" that led Jesus to feel abandoned on the cross ("Why have you forsaken me?") and the foreknowledge of this separation that led Jesus to be in such anguish in the garden of Gethsemane.

This is a compelling idea, but I believe it misrepresents what occurred on the cross and diminishes the character of God. While we speak of Jesus bearing the sins of the world on the cross, the idea is not that the Father literally covered Jesus with the world's sins. The idea is that the punishment those sins merited was voluntarily taken by Jesus on the cross (He suffered for sins he did not commit.) in order to reconcile us to God. There was no reason for the Father to turn away. This was, in fact, the greatest act of sacrificial love imaginable and part of God's own plan. God did not look away but instead looked with love and anguish at the suffering of his Son. God was grieved by it, seeing in the suffering and death of Jesus his Son's effort to draw the world to God. By watching this act, the Father joined in the suffering of the Son during those hours on the cross.

But why, then, was Jesus distressed and anguished? Let's consider several reasons, each of which offers insight into the meaning of Gethsemane.

### The "Why" of Jesus' Anguish

Jesus may have experienced anguish because he was wrestling once more with the tempter—the same tempter who sought to lead him away from the cross when he began his public ministry. Perhaps Jesus could hear the devil whispering, "Are you sure you are the Son of God? If you are not, you will be throwing your life away!" or maybe, "Would God really want his Son to die? Surely this cannot be his will; you have misunderstood." Maybe the tempter whispered, "Are you sure there is not some other way? You're only thirty-three! You've got so much more you could do with your life. Flee now; you still have time! Or simply tell them what they want to hear, and they will let you go!"

The mental and spiritual turmoil of such temptation would have been great. Jesus was being offered freedom from suffering. How easy it would have been to justify a decision to bypass the cross. Can you imagine the thoughts running through his mind? How many more could be touched if he lived? And the disciples—Look at them; they were sleeping! They were not ready to lead this work. What if the mission ended with the cross? Would it all have been for nothing?

Is it a coincidence that Jesus prayed three times for the cup to pass from him? Or was this meant to remind us of the three temptations in the wilderness (Luke 4:1-13)? We have already noted John's mention that Gethsemane was a garden, pointing us to Eden where others struggled and succumbed to the tempter. But here, in Gethsemane, as in the wilderness three years earlier, Jesus withstood the temptation, this time praying to his Father, "Not my will but yours be done" (Luke 22:42).

There is a second possible explanation for Jesus' anguish, or at least an additional element that added to it: his knowledge of Jerusalem's fate if the conflict with the Jewish leaders was brought to a head this way. If Jesus died, most people would not see him as the Messiah. They would continue to search for another. They would not understand that God wanted them to love their enemies, and they would await a messiah who could lead them in attempting to overthrow the Romans.

They would not have to wait long. Thirty years after Jesus' death and resurrection, those searching for a military messiah would find a man who would lead them in a war against the Romans. Roman reaction would be swift and furious. During the period from AD 66 to 73, the Romans would crush the Jewish people, killing over a million Jews and their supporters. Jerusalem would be laid waste, the Temple destroyed. Jesus knew this was in store for the Jewish people if he was crucified. Could this, too, have weighed heavily on his heart that night? Keep in mind that Jesus chose to pray in the garden of Gethsemane, from which he could look upon the Holy City. He could see the Temple from there, a temple that would be destroyed. If this seems a bit far-fetched, consider the only time in Luke's Gospel when Jesus wept. It occurred four days earlier, on Palm Sunday. Jesus was coming down the Mount of Olives. Here is how Luke describes the scene:

> As he came near and saw the city, he wept over it, saying, "If you, even you, had only recognized on this day the things that make for peace! But now they are hidden from your eyes. Indeed, the days will come upon you, when your enemies will set up ramparts around you and surround you, and hem you in on every side. They will crush you to the ground, you and your children within you, and they will not leave within you one stone upon another; because you did not recognize the time of your visitation from God." (Luke 19:41-44)

Recall that, just hours before, Jesus stood at the Temple Mount predicting that "not one stone will be left here upon another" (Matthew 24:2); and he offered his "little apocalypse," which described in such vivid detail the destruction of Jerusalem (Matthew 24). In the garden, he grieved not only for himself but also for what would happen to the city, as he asked whether he was truly meant to drink from this cup.

I believe these two explanations for Jesus' anguish may account for the mental suffering he experienced, but we dare not miss the obvious reason for his agony in the garden. Can we allow Jesus to be a person? Hasn't the church always asserted that in Jesus, God had become "fully human"? Did Paul not say that in Jesus the Son had "emptied himself" of his divinity in some meaningful sense (Philippians 2:7)? What would you be feeling if you knew that within a few hours you would be tortured; publicly humiliated; and then subjected to one of the cruelest, most inhumane and painful forms of capital punishment ever devised by human beings? What if you knew that your death would leave open the possibility that terrible atrocities would be committed that you might have prevented? Can you sense the anguish Jesus must have felt?

In the coming chapters we will explore the nature of the humiliation, torture, and death that awaited Jesus after he drank this cup. As a person, he had good reason to feel "deeply grieved, even to death" (Mark 14:34).

## "Not What I Want, But What You Want" (Mark 14:36)

Each of us knows what it is like to sense that God wants us to do something we do not want to do. We may feel called to take on a new ministry, to leave behind an unhealthy relationship, or to give a sacrificial gift to an organization. It may be a short-term or long-term call to the mission field, or it could be a call to serve and love others outside our comfort zone.

One of my parishioners felt called to teach the Alpha course, an introduction to Christian faith, in a federal penitentiary; but the first time she approached the security gates and barbed-wire fencing at Leavenworth Penitentiary and then entered to meet the federal prisoners, she was terrified and wanted to back out. Another parishioner felt God calling her to leave her corporate job to go into the mission field in Honduras. Another felt compelled to start a ministry to the homeless. Still another was certain God was calling him to adopt a child from foster care.

Each of these people had moments of anxiety related to answering God's call; and each ultimately prayed, as Jesus prayed, "Not what I want, but what you want." This prayer captures the essence of complete trust. It is bold enough to lay before God our desires and humble and obedient enough to reassert that we will do whatever God calls us to do, no matter the cost.

Among the prayers I offer most mornings is the Covenant Prayer in the Wesleyan Tradition. It begins, "I am no longer my own, but thine. Put me to what thou wilt..." In other words, "Not what I want, but what you want." This simple prayer of obedience and trust goes a long way toward bringing us peace. Through it, Jesus teaches us that it is acceptable to tell God what we hope and desire ("Remove this cup from me" [Mark 14:36b].) but that the final word in our prayer is to be simple trust and submission to God's will ("Yet, not what I want, but what you want" [Mark 14:36c].).

## Betrayed With a Kiss

Let us turn to the final part of this episode, which occurred sometime between one o'clock and three o'clock in the morning. At that time Judas, one of the Twelve, arrived in the garden, leading those sent by the religious authorities to arrest Jesus. By taking Jesus at night, the authorities avoided the potential of an uprising against them. Jesus knew the arrest was coming. He even knew that his friend Judas would betray him. But what must Jesus have felt when he saw Judas coming toward him? *Et tu, Brute?*

The imagery is so powerful that, two thousand years later, the name "Judas" continues to be synonymous with "traitor." Why did Judas betray Jesus? Much has been written on the subject. Some believe he sought to force Jesus to action, anticipating he would raise an army and lead the revolution Judas expected. Others believe he was disillusioned with Jesus, and still others believe he was simply greedy for gain. The Gospel writers do tell us that, whatever his motive, Judas was filled with grief following Jesus' arrest and trial and that he took his own life after the Crucifixion.

Judas is such a tragic figure; and each of us has been a Judas, both to Jesus and to others. It has been noted that Judas himself must have been conflicted and in agony on this night. The sign he chose by which he would betray Jesus was a kiss.

The Greek word for "kiss" that is used here is *philein,* a word used to describe true affection for another. Judas loved Jesus, but he was willing to betray him. He loved him, but he resented him. He loved him, but he was frustrated by him. He loved him, but he sold his friend for thirty pieces of silver.

Some have suggested that Jesus forgave Judas in the end and that Judas stands in heaven as the ultimate sign of the grace of God. Others disagree. What do you think? Had Judas asked for mercy from Jesus, would Jesus have given it?

As the arrest unfolded, Peter drew a sword and struck the high priest's servant's ear. (John identifies him by name, "Malchus" [John 18:10].) Luke the physician tells us that Jesus healed the man's ear (Luke 22:51), and I love this little fact. On the eve of his own torture and crucifixion, Jesus paused to heal a man sent to arrest him. He then commanded the disciples to put away their swords, saying, "For all who take the sword will perish by the sword" (Matthew 26:52b).

After the arrest, Jesus was bound by the club-wielding band. As their teacher was shackled, the disciples took flight. Mark tells us, in what some believe is an autobiographical allusion, that a young man who followed Jesus was with the disciples in the garden. As he fled, someone tried to seize him by his robe. He ran with such fervor that he left the robe behind and went naked into the darkness (Mark 14:51-52). Jesus stood watching as all his disciples deserted him. Only Judas remained. Jesus had been betrayed with a kiss, then deserted by his friends. And his suffering was only beginning.

# 3. Condemned by the Righteous

*They took Jesus to the high priest; and all the chief priests, the elders, and the scribes were assembled.... Now the chief priests and the whole council were looking for testimony against Jesus to put him to death.... The high priest asked him, "Are you the Messiah, the Son of the Blessed One?" Jesus said, "I am; and*

> *'you will see the Son of Man*
> *seated at the right hand of the Power,'*
> *and 'coming with the clouds of heaven.'"*

*Then the high priest tore his clothes and said, "Why do we still need witnesses? You have heard his blasphemy! What is your decision?" All of them condemned him as deserving death. Some began to spit on him, to blindfold him, and to strike him, saying to him, "Prophesy!" The guards also took him over and beat him.*

*While Peter was below in the courtyard, one of the servant-girls of the high priest came by. When she saw Peter warming himself, she stared at him and said, "You also were with Jesus, the man from Nazareth." But he denied it, saying, "I do not know or understand what you are talking about."... After a little while the bystanders again said to Peter, "Certainly you are one of them; for you are a Galilean." But he began to curse, and he swore an oath, "I do not know this man you are talking about." At that moment the cock crowed for the second time. Then Peter remembered that*

*Jesus had said to him, "Before the cock crows twice, you will deny me three times." And he broke down and wept. (MARK 14:53, 55, 61-68, 70-72)*

## Thursday After Midnight
## THE HOUSE OF THE HIGH PRIEST

FROM WHERE HE stood, Jesus could look across the Kidron Valley at the great wall of the Temple, where earlier in the week he had taught. The people in the crowds whose adulation rang so loudly in his ears on Sunday were asleep following their own Passover celebrations. The disciples who had shared his life since he called the first of them on the edge of a Galilean lake had fled during the chaos that accompanied his arrest. Now, bound hand and foot by Temple guards, Jesus was led back toward the city walls.

They passed again the tombs of the ancient priests—tombs that are still there—and the gates where the Book of Ezekiel says the Messiah will one day place his feet. They passed the Temple, far below the lofty pinnacle where, we are told, Jesus was tempted by the devil, who dared Jesus to cast himself down to prove, as the angels rushed to his aid, that he was indeed the Messiah. Down the valley they walked; then they began pushing and pulling Jesus up the hill of Zion, making their way through the lower City of David, which had been built over a thousand years earlier by that great king. They climbed the long stairway leading from the lower to the upper city—stairs that are still partially intact. Visitors may still walk on them, remembering and reenacting Jesus' journey this night. I have trod them, walking barefoot on those stones, imagining this very night. Finally, after a twenty-minute trek that had brought them about a mile from the garden, the guards led Jesus into the house of Caiaphas, the high priest. In the meantime, two of Jesus' disciples, Peter and John, had mustered enough courage to follow at a distance, hiding in the shadows, distraught and afraid.

## Jesus' Trial Before Caiaphas

Once Jesus was in custody, the Sanhedrin, or Jewish ruling council, was called hastily to the grand hall of what was no doubt a palatial home befitting the high priest. Today, on the spot where that home is believed to have stood is a church called Saint Peter Gallicantu—the latter being a Latin word meaning "cock crow." Below the ground is a prison cell, a cold stone pit fashioned from a cistern; and it is taught that this is where Jesus was held—lowered through a hole in the ceiling—first as the Sanhedrin debated his fate and again as he awaited transport to Pontius Pilate after sunrise. It is not hard to imagine Jesus in that pit praying the words of Psalm 88:1-4:

> O LORD, God of my salvation,
>     when, at night, I cry out in your presence,
> let my prayer come before you;
>     incline your ear to my cry.
>
> For my soul is full of troubles,
>     and my life draws near to Sheol.
> I am counted among those who go down to the Pit.

The Sanhedrin was a council comprised of seventy-one elders who were considered to be among the wisest and most pious men of the time. The very idea of the council comes from Numbers 11:16, where God commanded Moses to gather seventy leaders who would join him in governing the people on God's behalf. In Jesus' time, the seventy-one men ruled over the religious affairs of the people just as the Romans ruled over their political affairs. The Sanhedrin had control of the Temple and the religious courts. They were men who devoted themselves to God, and their high priest was the leading religious figure of his time.

The Sanhedrin normally met during the day in the Temple courts, and not during religious feasts. The fact that they were gathering in the high priest's palace, at night, during the feast of unleavened bread, points to both the unorthodoxy of the proceeding at hand and the urgency and secrecy they felt necessary in dealing with Jesus.

We need to step back from this scene for a moment to recognize its full import and appreciate its tragic irony. Christians believe that in Jesus, God walked in human flesh on this earth. He was in that sense like an emperor who so desires to know his subjects that he dons ordinary clothes and lives among them, with no one recognizing or understanding him. The God of the universe chose to walk in human flesh as an itinerant preacher, teacher, carpenter, healer—and pauper. He came as one of us. He healed the sick, forgave sinners, showed compassion to the lost, and taught people what God was really like. We must not miss the irony here: It was not the "sinners" who arrested God when he walked among us. Those who took him into custody and tried him were the most pious and religious people on the face of the earth. The God they claimed to serve walked among them in flesh, and they could not see him. They were so blinded by their love of power and their fear of losing it that they missed him. The people you would most expect to recognize and hail Jesus instead arrested him in darkness and brought him to trial. They put God on trial for blasphemy. Jesus' testimony that he was in fact the Messiah outraged them; and they found him guilty, convicting God of a crime worthy of the death penalty—blasphemy against himself! They spat on him, blindfolded him, and beat him (Mark 14:65). "Prophesy to us, you Messiah!" they yelled. "Who is it that struck you?" (Matthew 26:68). Then they turned him over to the guards to beat him again (Mark 14:65).

The question we are meant to ask, the question we *must* ask, is, "How could this happen?" How could seventy-one righteous men, dedicated to God, do what these men did? Why did they condemn an innocent man to death? And, even if they thought he was a false messiah, why would pious men, pillars of the community, spit on him? Why would they blindfold, mock, and strike him?

The answer, I believe, is fear. These men saw Jesus as a threat to their way of life, their positions of authority, their status among the Jews. They had seen the crowds flocking to him and had heard them say, "What is this? A new teaching—with authority! He commands even the unclean spirits, and they obey him" (Mark 1:27). Jesus threatened the very social order.

The reaction of Caiaphas the high priest was equal to that perceived threat. "This man is dangerous," we can imagine him saying. "If people continue to flock to him, the Romans are going to get wind of this; and who knows what they'll do to our people? This might actually lead to a great deal of pain for the entire nation, and certainly for us. It would be better for one man to die than for all the people to suffer. Jesus must die."

The idea was not a hard sell to the others. Their inherent fear and insecurity worked on them, ate at them; and fear breeds hate, which all too often leads to tragic acts of inhumanity. This part of the story is not simply about seventy-one supposedly pious Jewish men in the first century. This is about the human condition.

## Fear's Poisonous Work

We all are born afraid. Part of that is a mechanism God has given us to protect ourselves; we call it the self-preservation instinct. That mechanism can be helpful in dangerous situations. There are times when we have to fight, to work, to exert energy in order to save ourselves; and there also are times when we need to run from a situation. Unfortunately, our self-preservation instinct is coupled with our sin instinct. There is something in all of us that is broken. We have a propensity to do the wrong thing, to twist what was meant to be good, to misuse and distort it. You know this, and I know it.

As we look at the Sanhedrin and their treatment of Jesus, I would ask you to consider the ways the story relates to you. Fear performs its poisonous work within all of us. How often are we still motivated by it? In what ways does our fear lead us, individually and as a nation, to do what is wrong—what is at times unthinkable—while justifying our actions as necessary?

How was fear a part of the Salem witch trials in 1692 or of Joseph McCarthy's "Red Scare" in 1952? What role did fear play in the apartheid laws of South Africa or the Jim Crow laws of the United States? How did fear shape US foreign policy during the Cold War and after 9/11? How has your fear led you to do things you later regretted?

We each must be aware of the power of fear, and we must not forget the lessons of history. All of us, if we let our call to love be overshadowed by our innate fear, are capable of supporting and doing the unthinkable. When I read the story of Jesus' trial before the Sanhedrin, I am left wondering, "Would I have been among those who, out of fear and insecurity and the hate those feelings breed, found Jesus guilty of crimes worthy of death?"

I have heard some of my nonreligious friends say, "I'd believe in God if he would just show up, if he'd come and knock on my door." But God did that once, and this is what humanity did to him. Had you or I or my nonreligious friends been there, I am afraid we would have participated in these same things. I recognize myself in the Sanhedrin. I fear I would have made the same decision.

Preachers know about fear. It is easy to use fear to motivate people in the church, and that is something we have to be careful about. Politicians do it, also—just watch the ads they run. Unfortunately, those tactics too often work.

The question we must ask in our personal lives and in public policy as Christians is not "What is the thing that will make me feel most secure?" but "What is the most loving thing for me to do?" In the end, love conquers in ways that fear and hate and violence simply cannot. That is what the Scriptures teach us about the ways of God. I am reminded of this passage in First John:

> God is love, and those who abide in love abide in God, and God abides in them. Love has been perfected among us in this: that we may have boldness on the day of judgment, because as he is, so are we in this world. There is no fear in love, but perfect love casts out fear.... We love because he first loved us. Those who say, "I love God," and hate their brothers or sisters, are liars; for those who do not love a brother or sister whom they have seen, cannot love God whom they have not seen. (1 John 4:16b-20)

I am certain that at least a few of those seventy-one Sanhedrin members must have questioned whether putting Jesus to death was the right thing to do. Some had to wonder whether this man might not truly be the Messiah. But there is nothing in any of the Gospel accounts to indicate that a single one of them, other than Joseph of Arimathea, disagreed when it came to the death sentence they sought from Pilate. That points to another fact of human existence: Resisting those in leadership or in the majority, even when we believe they are doing wrong, is exceedingly difficult. When the tide is moving, we tend to be afraid to stand up and resist. I have seen this in myself from time to time. There have been occasions when people in authority said, "This is the way we ought to go," and I did not speak out for fear that doing so would make me look foolish. I have the feeling there were people in that Sanhedrin who later on said, "Why didn't I say anything?"

Martin Niemöeller, a Lutheran pastor in Nazi Germany during World War II, saw the sins being committed against the Jewish people and at first decided not to object. Only later did he begin to speak out against what he had seen. Words attributed to Niemöller movingly express his analysis of the situation: "First they came for the Communists and I didn't speak up because I wasn't a Communist. Then they came for the Jews and I didn't speak up because I wasn't a Jew. Then they came for the Catholics and I didn't speak up because I was a Protestant. Then they came for me and by that time there was no one left to speak up anymore."

I am also reminded of a quotation from the eighteenth-century British philosopher and politician Edmund Burke: "The only thing necessary for evil to triumph is for good men to do nothing."[1] Keeping silent, doing nothing when you see that something is wrong, is a sin.

No one spoke up in the Sanhedrin. No one asked, "Is this really in keeping with our faith?" How many times in recent history has the same thing happened—during the Holocaust, in Jim Crow America, in South Africa, at Abu Ghraib, and in your life and mine. How many times have we known something was wrong but were afraid to speak up? I am not talking about simply pointing out other people's sins. We all know Christians who freely point out the sins of others; they are not being courageous, just obnoxious. I am talking about those times when you are part of a group about to do something that is clearly wrong or when you see injustice being done to someone and all it would take would be one person speaking up, but everyone remains silent. What would have happened if one or two or three of those Sanhedrin members had simply said, "This isn't right, regardless of what we think about this man. It's not in keeping with what God teaches us." In our own situations we must be able to say, with great humility and despite our fear, "You know, this just doesn't feel right." In that pivotal moment when "Say something" and

"You dare not say anything" are both pounding in your head, say something.

## "I Am" (Mark 14:62)

At the center of the storm stood Jesus, listening as these "pious" men looked for reasons to put him to death. He saw their growing frustration as the witnesses they brought in to testify against him told varying stories. According to Jewish law, two people had to agree in their testimony in order to convict; and there was no agreement here. Finally, they looked at Jesus; and the high priest said, "Are you the Messiah, the Son of the Blessed One?" (Mark 14:61). All Jesus had to do was to keep silent, and there would have been no grounds for conviction; instead he replied in a manner deemed blasphemous for Jews and traitorous for Romans.

Jesus' response to this question of his identity brings together three Old Testament allusions, each of which assured his conviction by the Sanhedrin. Let's consider each of these. Jesus' first statement is easy to read as a simple, literal answer to the question, "Are you the Messiah?" Mark records it as two Greek words: "Ego eimi," or "I am" (Mark 14:62). Caiaphas, though, realized this was not a simple declarative. The straightforward answer would have been, "I am he," "I am the Blessed One," or even "I am the Messiah." But a simple "I am" in the Greek seems to point toward something much more profound. In John's Gospel the phrase has come to Jesus' lips time after time, so that scholars speak of the "I am" sayings of Jesus. The significance of these words likely goes back to a key passage in the Book of Exodus, where, 1200 years before Jesus, Moses saw a burning bush from which came the voice of God. When Moses asked God his name so he could tell it to the Israelites back in Egypt, God answered, "I AM WHO I AM" (Exodus 3:14). "I am" is therefore not simply the first-person singular of the verb "to be"; in Hebrew it is the personal name of God. In Hebrew, it was likely pronounced Yahweh, although it has often been mistranslated as Jehovah. In revealing this holy name to Moses, I believe God was saying, "I am the source of all life" and "Being itself comes from me."

By recording that Jesus' first statement to the high priest was "I am," I believe Mark intended for readers to see the connection between Jesus and his Father. Mark was stating what John records in the Prologue to his Gospel: "In the beginning was the Word, and the Word was with God, and the Word was God. He was in the beginning with God. All things came into being through him, and without him not one thing came into being. What has come into being in him was life, and the life was the light of all people" (John 1:1-4).

Because of Jesus' first statement, Caiaphas tore his clothes and deemed Jesus guilty of blasphemy. But Jesus was not finished. In a second statement he went on to say, "And 'you will see the Son of Man . . . coming with the clouds of heaven.'" (Mark 14:62), a reference to a passage beginning at Daniel 7:13. Jesus was counting on Caiaphas to fill in the rest of it:

> In my vision at night I looked, and there before me was one like a son of man, coming with the clouds of heaven. He approached the Ancient of Days and was led into his presence. He was given authority, glory and sovereign power; all nations and peoples of every language worshiped him. His dominion is an everlasting dominion that will not pass away, and his kingdom is one that will never be destroyed. (Daniel 7:13-14, TNIV)

Standing before the Sanhedrin, Jesus was identifying himself with the Messiah described in this passage from Daniel, noting that his glory—his rule over the entire earth—would come in the future, not in the present as the Jews had hoped. Jesus was saying that when the Messiah comes, he will rule; and God the

Father will grant him dominion, authority, and power over all people. His will shall be done, and on that day all nations and people will worship him—something reserved for God.

Jesus also said to Caiaphas that he would see the Son of Man "seated at the right hand of the Power" (Mark 14:62). That is an allusion to Psalm 110:1-4, where we read:

> The LORD says to my lord,
>   "Sit at my right hand
> until I make your enemies your footstool."
>
> The LORD sends out from Zion
>   your mighty scepter.
>   Rule in the midst of your foes.
> Your people will offer themselves willingly
>   on the day you lead your forces
>   on the holy mountains.
> From the womb of the morning,
>   like dew, your youth will come to you.
> The LORD has sworn and will not change his mind,
>   "You are a priest forever
>     according to the order of Melchizedek."

Twice in the Gospels we read that Jesus quoted this psalm (Matthew 26:64; Mark 14:62), likely written for and about David; and both times he applied it to himself, making himself prophetic heir of its promise. In this passage, the Lord (Yahweh) is speaking to Jesus, seating him at his right hand to rule. The enemies are those in that very room who will become his footstool. No doubt the members of the Sanhedrin again bristled as they recalled the psalm.

The reference to Melchizedek goes back 1600 years before the time of Jesus. Melchizedek was a king who had brought a meal of bread and wine to offer to Abraham, who had defeated Melchizedek's enemies in battle. The name "Melchizedek" in Hebrew means "King of Righteousness," and his act foreshadowed the bread and wine Jesus offers us in the Eucharist. Melchizedek is both king and priest, like Jesus who is the king of righteousness and who acts as priest, offering himself to God on behalf of the people. Jesus was identifying himself as the one foretold from the time of the psalmist and foreshadowed in the mysterious Melchizedek.

In this one sentence—three statements—Jesus testified that he was the Messiah, God's elect; and he alluded to a very special relationship between himself and God. Jesus was not merely a wonderful teacher. He was not merely a wonderworker. Nor was he the political messiah hoped for by the people. He understood himself to be closely associated with Yahweh, to be the promised Son of Man who would come again on the clouds, having been given rule over all people and seated at the right hand of God, serving as both priest and king. The Sanhedrin, learned enough to take in the full scope of Jesus' statements and claims, rent their clothes at the audacious enormity of it all and said, in effect, "Do we need any more witnesses? This man has blasphemed and is worthy of death." Jesus stood convicted.

## "I Do Not Know This Man" (Mark 14:71)

The final act in this part of the drama, meanwhile, was taking place in the courtyard, around a fire where Peter was warming himself. We know what is coming—Peter is going to deny Jesus, an act for which he is still remembered. But as easy as it is to look down on him for denying Jesus, as easy as it might be to see him as a coward, it is important to recognize the courage Peter had demonstrated up to that point.

When the guards came to arrest Jesus in the garden of Gethsemane, it was Peter who drew his sword and showed himself ready to fight a detachment of armed guards. In fact, he lopped off the ear of the high priest's servant. Jesus turned to Peter and said, "Put your sword back into its sheath. Am I not to drink the cup that the Father has given me?" (John 18:11). Peter may have been misguided, but he was the one courageous enough to try to fight for Jesus.

In the Gospels of Matthew, Mark, and Luke, we find that as Jesus was led away, the disciples fled—except for Peter. Peter followed the guards as they took Jesus to Caiaphas' house. He clung to the shadows; but when he got there, he steeled himself and entered the high priest's very courtyard to see what was happening. Do you see the courage it took to do that? Would you have walked into the courtyard knowing you could be put to death for being a disciple of Jesus?

Still, Peter's courage lasted only up to a point. Warming himself at the fire, he stood among the Temple guards as the trial went on; but he was probably doing his best to conceal his identity. Then, when a servant girl called attention to him, he began to waver. "You also were with that Nazarene, Jesus" she said. "I know you were" (Mark 14:67, TNIV). At that moment, fear took over. Knowing he was in danger of being harmed, Peter would not stand up as one of Jesus' disciples.

"I do not know or understand what you are talking about," he said (Mark 14:68); and he walked from the inner courtyard to the outer. The woman followed him and said again, in effect, "I know you were with him. I'm looking at you, and I know you were one of his disciples." And once more he denied it. Finally, a group of people who had been watching him, studying his easily identifiable Galilean accent, came up and said, "Surely you are one of them, for you are a Galilean" (Mark 14:70, TNIV).

Peter began calling curses from heaven upon himself, swearing to them, "I do not know this man you are talking about" (Mark 14:71). At that moment a rooster crowed for the second time, and Peter remembered what Jesus had said: "Before the cock crows twice, you will deny me three times" (Mark 14:72).

Luke tells us that at that instant, Jesus looked from inside the hall at Peter; and when their eyes met, this rugged lifelong fisherman, this rough-hewn leader of Jesus' disciples, broke down and wept (Luke 22:61-62).

The incident is one of the few that is mentioned in all Four Gospels, so all four writers must have considered it important. It was not included in order to embarrass Peter. The Gospels were written, in fact, after (tradition tells us) Peter had been crucified upside down for his faith. The Gospel writers knew the story because Peter must have regularly told the awful truth of that episode himself. None of the other disciples (except John) was there. Peter must have told it when he went to preach. Peter would surely have said, "I know you've denied Jesus. I denied him myself. I denied him in a way that I am deeply ashamed of, and yet I have to tell you: I betrayed the Lord, but he gave me grace. He took me back. And if you've denied him, he will take you back, too." Peter wanted to reassure others that, despite the fact that there are times when all of us deny the Lord, he will continue to take us back and use us to accomplish his work. From that moment forward, Peter would never again deny Jesus.

They say that when you visit the Holy Land, you will inevitably have a moment when you find yourself transported back in time to experience some part of the gospel story. For me this happened on the first night of my first trip to the Holy Land. It was March, about the time of year when Jesus was arrested. We were staying in a hotel atop the Mount of Olives, overlooking the Holy City, Jerusalem. I could not sleep; and though it was still dark, I got dressed, walked out in front of the hotel, and sat on a bench beneath an olive tree. I shivered in the cold and immediately began to think of Peter trying to warm himself at the fire in the high priest's courtyard. As I sat there lost in my thoughts, somewhere down the mount from the hotel, a cock began to crow. Suddenly my mind was filled with all the times I had denied

Jesus. I had denied him when I said and did things I knew were not in keeping with his will, when I engaged in thoughts and deeds that were counter to my faith, when I was more concerned with what others thought of me than with what he thought of me, when I was afraid to stand up and be counted as one of his disciples, or when I did something I knew was wrong because other people were calling me to do it. I sat there on the Mount of Olives in the cool, spring darkness and knew, for a moment, a taste of the grief and shame that brought Peter to tears.

We can learn something from each of the participants in Jesus' trial before Caiaphas. The members of the Sanhedrin clearly illustrate the human tendency to allow fear to make us do what we know is wrong. In their case, it was their condemnation of Jesus, their blindfolding and beating of him, and the silence of those who knew it was wrong. Jesus' testimony is meant to teach us about who Jesus was and is. He is more than a great teacher, more than a prophet. He is the "I AM," the Priest-King who will come one day on the clouds to reign over all. Peter's denial is a reminder that we who have answered the call to follow Jesus are tempted at times to deny even that we know him; and it serves as an invitation for us to be counted among his followers, regardless of the cost.

---

[1] Edmund Burke; see The Quotations Page, http://www.quotationspage.com/quotes/Edmund_Burke/. (March 14, 2006)

# 4. Jesus, Barabbas, and Pilate

*As soon as it was morning, the chief priests held a consultation with the elders and scribes and the whole council. They bound Jesus, led him away, and handed him over to Pilate. Pilate asked him, "Are you the King of the Jews?" He answered him, "You say so." Then the chief priests accused him of many things. Pilate asked him again, "Have you no answer? See how many charges they bring against you." But Jesus made no further reply, so that Pilate was amazed.*

*Now at the festival he used to release a prisoner for them, anyone for whom they asked. Now a man called Barabbas was in prison with the rebels who had committed murder during the insurrection. So the crowd came and began to ask Pilate to do for them according to his custom. Then he answered them, "Do you want me to release for you the King of the Jews?" For he realized that it was out of jealousy that the chief priests had handed him over. But the chief priests stirred up the crowd to have him release Barabbas for them instead. Pilate spoke to them again, "Then what do you wish me to do with the man you call the King of the Jews?" They shouted back, "Crucify him!" Pilate asked them, "Why, what evil has he done?" But they shouted all the more, "Crucify him!" So Pilate, wishing to satisfy the crowd, released Barabbas for them; and after flogging Jesus, he handed him over to be crucified. (MARK 15:1-15)*

## Friday Morning
### 7:00 AM
### ANTONIA FORTRESS

JUST AFTER DAYBREAK, Jesus was bound again and led away from the palace of the high priest. The spiritual leaders who made up the Sanhedrin had judged him guilty of blasphemy and decided he must die. Since they did not have the power to execute him (Capital punishment was a Roman prerogative.), they deliberated and decided to take him to someone who did have this power: Pontius Pilate, the Roman governor. They knew the charge of blasphemy would mean nothing to Pilate; but they also knew that if Jesus claimed to be the Messiah, he was claiming to be king, the Anointed One who would rule over the people. The Romans would take great interest in someone so obviously plotting insurrection. They had no patience for such people, who were invariably tortured and crucified.

So, as the sun rose over Jerusalem, Jesus was led through the streets to Pilate's Antonia Fortress, just a quarter of a mile away. The crowd that followed included the Sanhedrin and others who had been notified of Jesus' arrest, as well as his mother, his disciple John, and likely Peter. John (19:13) tells us that the name of the place where Jesus was to be tried was called the Stone Pavement (in Greek, *lithostrotos*). Did John record this name as a way of subtly pointing up one of the many ironies inherent in the events of this day? Only days before, Jesus had quoted Psalm 118:22 to describe the growing opposition to his teaching (Mark 14:10). The psalm says, "The stone [Greek, *lithos*] that the builders rejected / has become the chief cornerstone." And now the "stone" was being rejected by the Jewish leaders at the "stone pavement." Before the day was finished, Jesus would be laid to rest in a tomb hewn out of rock; and a large round stone would be placed at the entrance.

## The Suffering Servant

The Antonia Fortress was both the governor's residence and a military garrison in the heart of the city. It was adjacent to the Temple itself, and a Roman military presence so intimately tied to such a holy site both grieved and angered the Jewish people. On this chilly morning, though, the Sanhedrin was glad to have Pilate nearby to hear their case against Jesus. The Jewish authorities surely knew that Jesus had no intention of leading a rebellion against Rome; the only authority over which he expressed outrage was theirs as religious leaders. Still, their charges would either force Jesus to deny that he was the Messiah or, if he refused, force Pilate to put him to death for insurrection.

As he had at the trial before the Sanhedrin, Jesus remained virtually silent before Pilate, who was astounded at his unwillingness to defend himself. Pilate knew the chief priests were accusing Jesus out of envy—Jesus was becoming more popular than they were, and their fear and insecurity drove their hatred—but why, he wondered, wasn't Jesus defending himself? He was charged with claiming to be king of the Jews, a capital offense. Caesar was king of the Jews now, and claiming that title was a sign of rebellion. When Pilate asked Jesus, "Are you the King of the Jews?" (Mark 15:2a), Jesus gave a short and cryptic answer: "You say so" (Mark 15:2b). Jesus might have been saying, "Yes, of course, I am." He might have meant simply, "You have spoken, and I am not going to disagree with you." But he did not elaborate. In Matthew, Mark, and Luke, Jesus did not say another word to Pilate. And so, Pilate must have wondered, "Why isn't he speaking?"

When I read about Jesus' silence at his trials, I think in part of his resignation, or, better yet, his *determination* to die. He was not about to defend himself. He was not trying to get out of the death penalty. Jesus went to Jerusalem anticipating his execution, believing it was part of God's plan.

In my mind, it is indisputable that Jesus knew what was going to happen. He had prayed, "Father...remove this cup from me; yet, not what I want, but what you want" (Mark 14:36). He accepted his fate and then fell silent. I believe that as he stood before both the Sanhedrin and Pilate, Jesus may well have had in mind Isaiah 53, the passage about the great "suffering servant." Written hundreds of years before the time of Jesus, it speaks of an individual who would suffer for the sins of the nation of Israel. Many Jews believe Isaiah was writing in that passage about the nation of Judah, which would be punished for the sins of her people, carried away into Babylon, and for a time be utterly destroyed. Jesus knew Judah had played the part of the suffering servant, but he saw in this passage a foreshadowing of his own mission from God in his role as Messiah. The early church would see in Isaiah 53 a profound picture of the suffering and death of Jesus:

> All we like sheep have gone astray;
>     we have all turned to our own way,
> and the LORD has laid on him
>     the iniquity of us all.
>
> He was oppressed, and he was afflicted,
>     yet he did not open his mouth;
> like a lamb that is led to the slaughter,
>     and like a sheep that before its shearers is silent,
> so he did not open his mouth. (Isaiah 53:6-7)

Jesus often acted intentionally to point toward or fulfill certain Scriptures. He mounted a donkey on Palm Sunday to point to his identity as the Messiah, knowing Zechariah 9:9 spoke of a king entering Jerusalem in such a manner. At the trials, his silence may have been meant to lead his followers to consider the words of Isaiah 53 and to see in them a guide to his suffering and death.

Jesus was offering himself as a sacrificial lamb for the sins of the world. His death, Christians believe, was redemptive. It was purposeful. Jesus did not die a disillusioned prophet. He was not simply a great teacher put to death by the Romans. He chose to go to Jerusalem, anticipating and even predicting to his disciples his death. Christians believe that that death was the vehicle by which God saved the world. Isaiah painted the picture:

> Surely he has borne our infirmities
>     and carried our diseases;
> yet we accounted him stricken,
>     struck down by God, and afflicted.
> But he was wounded for our transgressions,
>     crushed for our iniquities;
> upon him was the punishment that made us whole,
>     and by his bruises we are healed. (Isaiah 53:4-5)

At the Last Supper, Jesus said, "Take, eat; this is my body" (Matthew 26:26). Then he said, "This is my blood of the covenant, which is poured out for many for the forgiveness of sins" (Matthew 26:28). He understood that his death would bring about our salvation. It is worth pausing to reflect on exactly how that happens. Theologians have long wrestled with how we are to understand the doctrine of the Atonement—that is, the at-one-ment of God and humankind, our reconciliation with God through Jesus' death on the cross. Most thoughtful people wrestle with the question. It is difficult for us to comprehend fully at first glance how the death of Jesus brings about our salvation; it is something of an enigma.

There are a variety of theories. No one of them is wholly adequate, but taken together they paint a powerful and profound picture of the significance of Jesus' suffering and death for us. One theory of the Atonement teaches that Jesus suffered and died in place of humanity. He bore the punishment all of us deserve for our sins and in doing so offered grace and pardon for humankind. This theory is called the substitutionary theory of the Atonement, and we will discuss it again in a moment.

Some have dismissed the substitutionary theory of the Atonement as simplistic or even confusing, but for many it is the clearest way to understand what Jesus intended to happen as a result of his death on the cross. In the trial before Pontius Pilate we get a glimpse of this idea—one concrete example of a larger idea. For here at the *lithostrotos* Jesus took the place of a "notorious criminal" named Barabbas, who was himself awaiting death. Barabbas, a convicted criminal, was set free; and Jesus, an innocent man, was crucified in his place.

## The Costliness of Grace

Barabbas is intriguing both as a character in his own right and in his role in the death of Jesus. In Barabbas, we have an insurrectionist who led a revolt against the Romans; someone who apparently had murdered Roman collaborators, perhaps even Roman citizens; and a person who robbed others and presumably used their money for his cause.

It was custom for Pontius Pilate to release one prisoner to the Jewish people each year during the Passover. Timed to coincide with this celebration of the Jews' collective release from bondage in Egypt, it was a politically astute act of mercy meant to appease the multitudes and take some of the air out of the desire for rebellion. On this day, Pilate had two prisoners before him: Jesus of Nazareth and Barabbas. Both were charged with leading insurrections and with wishing to be king of the Jews. Pilate turned to the people and said, "Which of the two do you want me to release for you?" (Matthew 27:21). Would it be Barabbas, who had robbed and murdered, or Jesus of Nazareth, who had done nothing wrong—the Jesus who loved lost people, taught them about the kingdom of God, healed the sick, and blessed many?

Pilate apparently thought the people would ask for Jesus, and he was all too happy to oblige; but they asked instead for Barabbas, and in the end it was Barabbas he released. In Mel Gibson's film *The Passion of the Christ,* as Barabbas was released, he looked back upon Jesus; and a momentary look of understanding crossed his face. For an instant, Barabbas seemed to comprehend that this innocent man would be nailed to the cross in his place. Barabbas would be the first sinner for whom Jesus died. This is one small picture of the substitutionary work of atonement Jesus performed with his death; for we, like Barabbas, have been spared, with Jesus suffering the punishment we deserve.

The substitutionary theory of the Atonement, which we touched on before, can be summarized in this way: Every one of us has sinned, and in our sin we have been alienated from God. Justice calls for punishment for the collective weight of that sin; the Bible says that "the wages of sin is death" (Romans 6:23) and eternal separation from God. But God, who loves us like parents love their children, does not desire us to be eternally separated. God wishes us to receive grace. An ordinary person could not die for all humankind; but Jesus, being God in the flesh, could die for the sins of the entire world. He paid a price he did not owe, giving us a gift of grace we did not deserve. This is what we see in Barabbas walking away free from the prison and Jesus hanging on a cross.

This theory is confusing for many. It undoubtedly was easier to grasp in a day when animals were routinely sacrificed to atone for sin. Today we think that we are not that bad, that we do not really need Jesus to die on the cross for us. Some of us feel that sin does not require sacrifice or atonement. But there are moments when the idea of Christ's death being *for us* comes into focus, moments when we have done something so awful and our shame is so great that we know there is no way we can save ourselves. It is in those moments when we find ourselves drawn to the cross and the understanding that Christ suffered for us. We look at the cross and realize that a price was already paid for us.

I am reminded of the story of an individual who was driving drunk and ran across the median, hitting another car and killing a child in that car. He was jailed for manslaughter, but no amount of jail time could bring back the life of that child. This man spent the rest of his life punishing himself for the crime he had committed. If only he had known the price had been paid, that the punishment had already been borne by Jesus Christ.

We are meant to look at the cross and see both God's great love and the costliness of grace and to find our hearts changed by what God has done for us. We are meant, as a result of understanding that cost, to serve God with humble gratitude, and to long, as we see Jesus suffer, never to sin again. And yet, of course, we will sin again and call again upon the grace of God revealed on the cross. Like Barabbas, we walk away free because of the suffering of an innocent man.

## Looking for a Messiah

Barabbas is not the only character we are meant to identify with as we consider this story. We are meant to see ourselves in the crowd, too. Apparently, these people started gathering at six o'clock in the morning to call for Jesus' crucifixion. Often, we think of that crowd and associate it with all the Jews in Jesus' day. I have to tell you, that is absolutely wrong! Not all the Jews wanted Jesus crucified. The crowd outside the Antonia Fortress was probably a relatively small one, perhaps dozens or a few hundred people at the most. There were many others who believed in Jesus, who trusted in him, who thought he was a profound teacher and a wonderworker and appreciated his words. But there were some who did not.

Some of the people in that early morning crowd were no doubt merchants and moneychangers from the Temple courts. Just a few days earlier, Jesus had turned over their tables and thrown them out of the Temple. They had been humiliated and had lost revenue. This morning they were standing in front of the fortress saying, in effect, "Jesus deserves whatever he gets here. Did you see what he did to us? He ruined our business. He deserves to die!" Then there were probably those who were just thugs and rabble-rousers, people who enjoyed seeing violent things happen.

No doubt there were people in the crowd who were neither disgruntled merchants nor thugs. Many of these people must have been present when Jesus came down from the Mount of Olives on the day we now call Palm Sunday. They had waved their palm branches before him and shouted,

> Hosanna!
> Blessed is the one who comes in the name of the Lord!
> Hosanna in the highest heaven! (Mark 11:9)

Now, on Friday, they were shouting, "Crucify him!" Why? How can people change so suddenly and so drastically?

To understand, we need to look at who the people thought Jesus was and what they thought he was going to be like. When he rode into town on the donkey and they welcomed him in a palm-waving frenzy, the people on that first Palm Sunday were harking back to a similar episode 190 years earlier, when another government oppressed the Jews. That had been the Greek Seleucid dynasty, which had killed many of the Jewish people and, in the midst of their oppression, set up an altar to Zeus in the Jewish Temple and slaughtered pigs on it.

Then, in 165 BC, a family of Jews, the Maccabees, brought together enough like-minded compatriots to incite an insurrection. They routed the Greeks and forced them out of Jerusalem and the Holy Land. They cleansed the Temple, an occasion our Jewish friends still celebrate as Hanukkah. When Simon Maccabee returned to Jerusalem, he was hailed as the great deliverer; and the people took palm branches and waved them in front of him as a sign of victory. "You have freed us from the Greeks," they cried. "Hail to you."

The idea of waving palm branches for Simon Maccabee and the deliverance of Jerusalem was likely drawn from the Festival of Tabernacles or Booths, called *Succoth*. During this annual week-long feast, the Jewish people were commanded to remember their sojourn in the wilderness. Each day the people would wave branches as a part of their celebration. On the last day of the feast, a day called Hosanna Rabbah, the people would circle the altar at the Temple seven times, offering up prayers of "Hosanna"—a word that is loosely translated as "Save us now!" On this day the people would ask God to deliver them. They would recite the words of Psalm 118:26, "Blessed is he who comes in the name of the LORD," as they contemplated God's future deliverance of his people. Simon's entrance into Jerusalem as deliverer was seen as an answer to the prayers offered annually during the Feast of Tabernacles.

So when the Jews waved palm branches as Jesus came down from the Mount of Olives, they were saying, "Jesus, be our deliverer. Save us from the Romans (as Simon saved our forebears). Cast out our enemies, and free us from their awful oppression." That is what they were looking for in Jesus: a messiah, which means "anointed one" or king. David was a messiah. Solomon was a messiah. Any of the ancient kings anointed by the priests were said to be messiahs. We can see, therefore, that these people had very specific expectations about what the Messiah would be like.

During the years between Jesus' birth and the destruction of Jerusalem by the Romans in AD 70, at least eight people, and perhaps as many as thirteen, called themselves messiah or were hailed as messiah by some of the Jewish people. Josephus, the first-century Roman historian, tells us about a few of them. Some were murderers and thieves. Some were earnest in their desire to reign for God. Some gathered a dozen followers, or maybe a few hundred. In the case of one man, six thousand people joined him to become a fighting force. Every one of these would-be messiahs used the sword in trying to drive out the Romans and establish a new kingdom of Israel. Each understood this to be the task of the Messiah, as did the people. And every one of these supposed messiahs was sentenced to death.

When Jesus came into Jerusalem, many were anticipating a messiah who would lead an armed rebellion against the Romans; and he sorely disappointed them. Jesus was the only messiah who refused to take up the sword. He had no interest in inciting crowds to throw off the shackles of Roman oppression. Instead, he taught people to love their enemies and pray for their persecutors. He called blessed those who suffer for what is true and right, those who are meek, those who are peacemakers. If a Roman soldier forces you to carry his pack a mile, Jesus told them, carry it the second mile. If a Roman strikes you on the cheek, turn the other toward him.

This was not what the people were looking for. Here was a would-be messiah who went against everything many of them believed in. For them, the only way to survive was by force. Freedom required the sword. But Jesus said, in effect, "Listen; I tell you: It is not by the power of the sword but by the power of the cross that you will be free. It's not going to be by raising up an army to fight the Romans. Rather, it will be by demonstrating sacrificial love." And he was right. Jesus knew that even if every Jewish man, woman, and child of his day were armed to the teeth and pitted against the Romans, they would still be crushed. He knew the little land of Judah, even with the aid of Galilee and Samaria, could not defeat the power of imperial Rome.

Jesus realized that victory over the Romans would not come by way of the sword. He said it would come by the power of *agape*—a sacrificial love that ultimately cannot be defeated. "You will conquer them," he was saying in effect, "with the power of an idea. When they hear about your God and see that God lived out in your lives, their hearts will be changed."

That, of course, is just what happened. The Romans, by and large, no longer worshiped with any passion the tired gods they had venerated for so long. When Christians began to talk of a God who walked on this earth as a humble carpenter, who suffered and died for his own people, and then, in final victory, was raised from the dead, they found the idea so captivating that they began to follow Jesus. Christianity spread among the slaves and common people and even to some extent among the upper classes. The story of a God who came as a man to call people to love and who suffered for them was a far more powerful story than any to be found among the Greco-Roman pantheon of gods. The Roman Empire was ultimately conquered not by the sword, but by the cross of Christ. This was the way of Jesus. Yet on this fateful day, as Jesus stood before the Roman governor, with the religious leaders, merchants, and an assortment of common people at his back, there was no one who as yet understood.

## The Legacies of Jesus and Barabbas

Pilate stood before the early morning crowd offering them a choice. They would be permitted to request the release of one would-be messiah while condemning the other to death.

Matthew tells us Barabbas' name was actually "Jesus Barabbas" (Matthew 27:16). The name "Barabbas" means "son of the Father," and the name "Jesus" means "Savior"; so Matthew makes clear the crowd was being given a choice between two messianic figures. If you picture yourself as part of that crowd, which one do you pick? One is going to lead by force; throw out the Romans; reclaim your tax money, wealth, and prosperity; and restore the strength of the Jewish kingdom. The other's leadership involves loving these same oppressors, serving them as they dwell among you, doubling the service they demand of you. Whom do you wish to see freed? Whom do you wish to see destroyed?

When we see the choice in that way, it is not so difficult to understand the crowd's choice of Barabbas over Jesus. They chose the path of physical strength, military might, and lower taxes over the path of peace through sacrificial love.

History offers us a recent example of this choice in the approaches of Malcolm X and Martin Luther King, Jr., to the civil rights struggles of the 1950s and 1960s. Both leaders wanted to ensure justice and equal rights for people of color, but their methodologies differed radically. Malcolm X believed the injustice was so serious that violence was sometimes justified in overcoming it. His approach is illustrated by this 1964 quote: "I am for violence if non-violence means we continue postponing a solution to the American black man's problem just to avoid violence. I don't go for non-violence if it also means a delayed solution. To me a delayed solution is a non-solution. Or I'll say it another way. If it must take violence to get the black man his human rights in this country, I'm for violence exactly as you know the Irish, the Poles, or Jews would be if they were flagrantly discriminated against."[1] It was only after a pilgrimage to his holy land that he began to question that approach, and he died a year later.

Dr. King, on the other hand, believed that human rights and equality come only by changing people's hearts through encounters with nonviolent resistance and sacrificial love. His approach, laid out in his sermon "Strength to Love," might be paraphrased as follows: "Our approach will be to shame you into giving us civil rights. We are going to show you, by our willingness to suffer, a different way. You can hurt us and hurt us and hurt us, and we are still going to love you. We are not going to hurt you physically, but we are going to stand up for what we believe is right. As you inflict suffering on us, we will wear you down with our capacity to endure. We will win victory by demonstrating love rather than hate toward you."

When it came to civil rights, what was it that finally changed our country? Was it violence and hate, or was it the power of sacrificial love? Both approaches had their advocates. Dr. King's approach mirrored the gospel and, I believe, led to an entire generation of whites whose hearts were changed as they witnessed the nonviolent resistance of his followers.

A generation earlier, Mahatma Gandhi had provided lessons and inspiration for Dr. King. Faced with war between Muslims and Hindus, he announced a hunger strike. "I am not going to eat," he said, "until these people stop fighting"; and this quiet and tiny man nearly starved himself to death before leaders of the two sides approached him and said, "Please, Mr. Gandhi. We will stop fighting if you will please start eating." This was the power of one man who, by the superiority of his ideas and his willingness to suffer, induced two peoples to pause in their warring.

How far could such an approach be taken today? Is it possible to live as Jesus of Nazareth urged in our own world? Could a nation or government even survive that way? I do know that Jesus asks us to choose his way over the way of Barabbas; but I also know that while many admire Jesus of Nazareth, they feel safer with, and prefer, Jesus Barabbas. That was the choice

Pilate gave the crowd two thousand years ago: the popular revolutionary Jesus Barabbas, who would change the world through power, or Jesus of Nazareth, who would change the world through sacrificial love. The crowd shouted, "Release Barabbas for us!" (Luke 23:18). Had you been standing there that day, whom would you have chosen?

## "Wishing to Satisfy the Crowd" (Mark 15:15)

We have pictured ourselves as Barabbas, a sinner set free by Jesus Christ. We have seen ourselves in the crowd, calling for his release rather than the release of Jesus. I believe we are also meant to see ourselves in Pontius Pilate, another truly compelling character. Pilate was procurator, or governor, of Judea from AD 26 to 36. Outside the New Testament, he is mentioned in just two first-century sources. Philo of Alexandria, a Jewish philosopher, quotes another source who described Pilate as "a man of inflexible disposition, harsh and stubborn."[2] Josephus, the Jewish historian, tells us that when Pilate met resistance to the idea of building an aqueduct for Jerusalem with Jewish taxes, he plundered the Temple to fund it.[3]

Luke 13:1 tells us how some Galileans came to the Temple to offer sacrifices (perhaps with the idea of leading the people in insurrection) and how Pilate killed them and mixed their blood with that of their sacrifices. Josephus says Pilate also slaughtered followers of a Samaritan who seemed to be claiming to be a prophet—an episode that led Rome to relieve Pilate of his governorship.[4]

Obviously, this was not a man who was hesitant about killing Jews. Still, when Jesus—a man claiming to be the king of the Jews—was brought before him, Pilate could not seem to bring himself to order his execution. Pilate was troubled by this man; we see this in each of the Gospels. Pilate apparently knew the reason Jesus had been brought before him was that the chief priests were envious. Pilate seemed to know that putting Jesus to death was wrong. (Some scholars point out, however, that the Gospels were written when Christianity was making inroads in the Roman Empire. Therefore these accounts may have emphasized Pilate's reluctance to crucify Jesus in order to make clear that Jesus had not been leading an insurrection against Rome.)

Mark tells us that Pilate wanted to release Jesus, saying, "What should I do with this man? I don't see any reason to kill him" (paraphrase of Mark 15:9-14). In Matthew, we find Pilate's wife pleading with him to have nothing to do with Jesus' death; for she had had a troubling dream about him (Matthew 27:19). Pilate thus pressed the crowd to call for the release of Jesus of Nazareth. But they continued to demand Jesus' crucifixion and the release of Barabbas.

Matthew then tells us Pilate washed his hands and said to the crowd, "I am innocent of this man's blood; see to it yourselves" (Matthew 27:24). Luke (23:6-12) says Pilate was sufficiently disturbed that he sent Jesus to King Herod Antipas, the ruler of Galilee, who happened to be in Jerusalem. Even though he treated Jesus "with contempt," Herod (the son of Herod the Great) likewise found no reason to kill Jesus and sent him back. John tells us Pilate had Jesus flogged in hopes that would satisfy the crowd, presenting to them a tattered and bloody Jesus. "Here is your King!" he told them. "Shall I crucify your King?" (John 19:14-15). As many as five or six times, John tells us, Pilate looked for a way to avoid crucifying Jesus; but the crowd would have none of it.

Until the end, Pilate had the authority and the inclination to set Jesus free. After all his hesitation, after all his resistance to the idea of crucifying Jesus, though, we come to one of the saddest lines in the account of Jesus' passion: "So Pilate, wishing to satisfy the crowd, released Barabbas for them; and after flogging Jesus, he handed him over to be crucified" (Mark 15:15). *Wishing to satisfy the crowd.* Pilate knew it was wrong. He had the power to stop it. But the pull of the crowd was compelling, just as the voice of the leaders had proven compelling to the Sanhedrin members who might have questioned their part in Jesus' death. Pilate sent Jesus to the cross to satisfy the clamor of the fickle and unruly mob in front of him.

Do you see yourself in Pontius Pilate? Each of us surely has played the part he played. From the time we were small, we have known the pull of the crowd. As adults, we feel it in a variety of ways—in our desire for acceptance, in our fear of ridicule and rejection. Our inability to think for ourselves leaves us silent when we should speak, leaves us doing or supporting things we know are wrong.

What have you done that you have known to be wrong simply because "the crowd" was clamoring for you to do it? What might you be willing to do if their pressure was intense enough? And who is your crowd? Not long ago a young man came to my office. He had gone off to college and found himself caught up in drugs, alcohol, and other things. He was a great kid, and I wanted to know what had happened. It was simple: His new friends were all doing these things; and, like Pilate, the young man had decided to "satisfy the crowd."

All of us experience it. Our whole culture is moving in one direction; and we find ourselves drawn in, doing things we know are not right, things we know are against God's will. Part of the reason gathering in church is so important is that for at least an hour every week we are surrounded by a crowd desiring to follow Jesus. It feels good to be among people who think the way we think and who encourage us. We draw strength from one another to keep walking the right path. This crowd, like the young man's friends, has a voice strong enough that it is hard to resist. We can be swayed by a crowd for good or for ill; so it is critical, if only for an hour on Sundays, to be surrounded by friends who share our values, convictions, and faith.

In a country where you will never be arrested for being a Christian, where you will never be put to death for following Jesus, are you willing in the face of a little peer pressure to be counted as one of his followers?

[1] From *The Autobiography of Malcolm X*, by Malcom X (Ballantine Books, 1964); page 402.

[2] See Livius: Articles on Ancient History, Pontius Pilate; http://www.livius.org/pi-pm/pilate/pilate04.html. (May 26, 2009)

[3] From *Thrones of Blood: A History of the Time of Jesus 37 B.C. to A.D. 70* (Barbour Publishing, Inc., 1993); page 61.

[4] From *Thrones of Blood: A History of the Time of Jesus 37 B.C. to A.D. 70*; page 62.

# 5. The Torture and Humiliation of the King

*After flogging Jesus, [Pilate] handed him over to be crucified.*

*Then the soldiers led him into the courtyard of the palace (that is, the governor's headquarters); and they called together the whole cohort. And they clothed him in a purple cloak; and after twisting some thorns into a crown, they put it on him. And they began saluting him, "Hail, King of the Jews!" They struck his head with a reed, spat upon him, and knelt down in homage to him. After mocking him, they stripped him of the purple cloak and put his own clothes on him. Then they led him out to crucify him.*

*They compelled a passer-by, who was coming in from the country, to carry his cross; it was Simon of Cyrene, the father of Alexander and Rufus. Then they brought Jesus to the place called Golgotha (which means the place of a skull). And they offered him wine mixed with myrrh; but he did not take it. (MARK 15:15b-23)*

## Friday Morning
### 8:00 AM
### ANTONIA FORTRESS

IT IS WORTH lingering on the last hours before Jesus' crucifixion, trying to understand more clearly the torture he underwent and what it might say about our own lives as we seek to follow him. The Gospels differ somewhat in their accounts of these hours. Luke mentions neither the flogging nor the mockery Jesus suffered at the hands of the Roman soldiers; but he alone tells us Pilate sent Jesus to Herod Antipas, son of Herod the Great and ruler of Galilee, where Jesus had lived. Herod happened to be in Jerusalem, and Pilate sought to shift responsibility for a verdict to him. Luke tells us that Herod questioned Jesus at length; and when Jesus refused to reply, Herod treated him contemptuously, mocking him and placing an "elegant robe" (Luke 23:11) on him before sending him back to Pilate, who sentenced him to crucifixion.

John's Gospel, the most familiar to many people and the one that served as the basis for Mel Gibson's *The Passion of the Christ,* tells us that Pilate sent Jesus to be flogged before passing sentence on him. Pilate seemed to hope the Jewish leaders would see flogging as sufficient punishment and drop their demands for Jesus' crucifixion. The soldiers flogged and mocked Jesus, placing a crown of thorns upon his brow and dressing him in a purple robe before bringing him back to Pilate, bloodied and humiliated. Pilate presented Jesus to the crowd; but unmoved to pity, they once more called for his crucifixion.

Matthew and Mark tell us Jesus was flogged, *then* taken away by the Roman guards, who led him into the governor's headquarters, where they mocked and humiliated him before taking him to be crucified. All but Luke agree that Jesus was flogged, and all four Gospels include some degree of mockery and humiliation. Still, this torture and humiliation are mentioned only briefly. What they mention in passing, we will consider in some detail in this chapter.

## Physical Torture: Flogging

Flogging was common in Jesus' day. Jews as well as Romans sometimes utilized it, as have cultures around the world and across time. It is the practice of striking someone with a whip or stick for punishment or torture. An old-fashioned whipping with a belt, often used on children before the "time out" concept came into fashion, was a form of flogging. In the past, many American prisons practiced flogging, as did the military during the Revolutionary War. Many governments still adhere to the practice, and only recently the news reported that a man in Iran was publicly flogged just before he was put to death.

The Romans used a lighter form of flogging on some lesser criminals; but when they wished to instill terror, they used methods so brutal that all but the most hardened spectators would turn away. Such beatings had, as you might guess, a great deterrent effect. In one form of Roman flogging, the victim was stripped and forced to bend over a post to which he was strapped, his hands tied down. Two or more lictors (Roman bodyguards who were specially trained in the art of inflicting pain through flogging) took turns striking the victim with whips. The flagrum or whip was made of leather, braided with bits of stone, metal, glass, bone, or other sharp objects specially designed to tear as well as bruise flesh. One variation of the whip, called "the scorpion," had nail-like talons even more efficient at tearing flesh from bone. The third-century church historian Eusebius said that in Roman flogging, often "the sufferer's veins were laid bare and the very muscles and tendons and bowels of the victim were open to exposure."[1]

Prisoners sometimes died before they ever made it to their crucifixions. Part of the cruelty inherent in flogging, though, was that such deaths were the exception. Flogging was designed to inflict incredible pain and damage but to leave the victim with just enough strength to carry his cross to the crucifixion site.

The accounts of Jesus' torture and humiliation follow closely the words of Isaiah 50:6, part of one of the "suffering servant" songs, seen by early Christians as pointing to Jesus' suffering at the hands of the Romans. These are verses Jesus would have had in mind as he faced these soldiers:

> I gave my back to those who struck me,
>   and my cheeks to those who pulled out the beard;
> I did not hide my face
>   from insult and spitting.

Some scholars believe passages such as this refer to the nation of Judah, personified in the figure of the suffering servant. But many of the verses regarding the suffering servant seem to point beyond Judah to what Jesus experienced on this terrible day. To me, some of the servant songs in Isaiah only make sense with reference to Jesus.

### Emotional Torture: Humiliation

Jesus did not beg for mercy. He did not demonstrate any of the behaviors expected of someone being flogged, and that no doubt angered the soldiers administering his punishment. They were not content to tear his flesh; they decided to dehumanize him, to break his spirit. Mark tells us, "Then the soldiers led him into the courtyard of the palace...and they called together the whole cohort" (Mark 15:16). A cohort typically consisted of 300 to 600 soldiers. The entire contingent, perhaps all those stationed in the Antonia Fortress, came out for some sport at the expense of the prisoner, who they knew had been accused of seeking to lead a rebellion against their emperor and claiming to be king.

Matthew tells us they stripped him naked, leaving him exposed and vulnerable, a bloodied, weakened man surrounded by hundreds of Rome's finest, their swords, shields, and armor all testament to the Empire's strength and resolve. Their emperor was, after all, king of the world; they would show this prisoner what they thought of his claim.

They decided to hold a mock coronation; and they brought him a robe, probably one of the soldiers' own robes. Matthew says it was red. Mark tells us it was purple, the color of royalty. Purple is to this day the liturgical color of the seasons of Advent, when we celebrate the coming birth of the King, and Lent, in which the church prepares for his death. Whatever the color, it was not a robe that would have concealed his nakedness. Draped over his shoulders, it would simply have covered his bloody back. The soldiers decided their freshly robed king needed a crown, and they twisted a branch from a thorn tree into a rough oval that parodied the royal laurel wreath. Then they pressed it down onto his brow in mock coronation so that the thorns dug into his flesh.

"Hail, King of the Jews!" (Matthew 27:29; Mark 15:18; John 19:3), they shouted, saluting him. Matthew tells us they took a reed—probably the equivalent of a cattail—and placed it in his hands as a mock scepter, a parody of the king's rod of authority. They approached and circled him, spitting on him and striking him in the face. They took the reed and used it to lash him, not so much to inflict pain, but to add to his humiliation. Some knelt before him, still shouting, "Hail, King of the Jews!"

It is this picture, this shamefully cruel and inhumane sport at the expense of a tormented man, that we need to fix on; for it is here that we get a clear and tragic glimpse of what humanity did when God took on flesh and walked among us. Jesus could have destroyed them all with a word. Instead, he bore the shame and humiliation, in part so that all who came after him could learn from this story something about the human condition and about the costliness of God's grace.

We must ask ourselves why the soldiers did these things. Why did they torture him? Why did they humiliate him? This man had loved lost people. He had preached the good news of the kingdom of God. He had healed the sick. He had opened the eyes of the blind. Of course, he had also challenged the authority of the religious leaders and pointed out their hypocrisy.

What kind of men were these? In every part of the story we have met people who did things that are difficult to imagine: the Sanhedrin demanding that Jesus be put to death; the crowd crying out for him to be crucified; Pontius Pilate sentencing him to satisfy the crowd; and the Roman soldiers taking delight in tearing the flesh from his bones, then spitting on and humiliating him.

Were all these hundreds of soldiers evil? Or did their role as occupiers in a foreign land, their constant awareness of the desire of the locals to be rid of them, bring out this inhumanity?

## The Evil Within Us

As I read and reread the Gospel accounts of soldiers stripping Jesus and tormenting him, I was reminded of the images of the Abu Ghraib prison, where during the Iraq War, American soldiers stripped Iraqis naked, mocked them, humiliated them, and photographed their handiwork. What could possibly lead men and women to do such things? Were they bad people, or did their circumstances somehow bring out this behavior? Are there times when we as ordinary people lose our humanity and, in our fear, find ourselves supporting policies and practices that in other, better times we would have resisted?

I have invited you at each step to see yourself in the story, and I invite you now to see yourself in the Roman soldiers. Doing so will help us recognize that human beings throughout history have been capable of inhumanity toward one another. Painfully enough, it is the story of our existence. In Noah's day, God was so grieved at the violent way people treated each other that he sent floodwaters to destroy the earth. It is easy for us to say, "I could never do that. I would never have been one of the Roman soldiers who took delight in mocking, lashing, and terrorizing an innocent man." We need to be careful about such claims.

In 1971, Philip Zimbardo, a psychologist at Stanford University, conducted a study for the United States Navy regarding the behavior of people in prisons. He and his colleagues transformed the basement of the psychology building at Stanford into a prison and hired twenty-four middle-class Stanford students, randomly assigning twelve to be guards and twelve to be prisoners. The latter were arrested and brought to the "prison," where they and their guards would be observed for fourteen days. But the experiment had to be called off after the sixth day because the college students chosen to be guards took to their roles so enthusiastically that they began to hurt and oppress their student prisoners. They had lost sight of the fact that it was an experiment.[2]

Zimbardo spent the next thirty years analyzing the results and studying what they might mean in other areas. What he found is that all of us—every one of us—are capable of being transformed from Dr. Jekyll into Mr. Hyde. He interviewed a Rwandan woman who was convinced by tribal leaders that her neighbors, people she had grown up with and known her whole life, were the enemy and needed to be destroyed. She killed the children and then the woman who was her longtime friend. She was unable to explain how or why it happened. She was ashamed of what she did, yet somehow she had undergone that transformation.[3]

In 1963, Stanley Milgram at Yale University invited people to come in off the street to take part in a scientific investigation. They were paid four dollars for one hour in which they were set in front of gauges and dials and told to deliver shocks when someone in the other room gave wrong answers to questions they were asked. The experiment was designed to see how far people would go if an authority figure told them they must go on increasing the force of the shock until it reached apparently fatal levels. No one was actually shocked; but the subjects did not know that, since they could hear but not see the person they supposedly were shocking. Before the experiment, researchers estimated just one percent of the US population would administer what they thought were lethal doses of electricity. What the researchers found was that sixty-five percent of the subjects were willing to increase the electricity to four hundred fifty volts, despite the apparent cries of pain coming from the person in the other room. Even after the cries finally fell silent, the subjects were still willing to give electrical jolts to that person because an authority figure told them they must complete the experiment. *Sixty-five percent!*[4]

As Zimbardo looked back at Milgram's experiment and his own, he recognized many historical parallels. Have you ever wondered what was so different about the Germans of the 1930s and 1940s? Were they so unlike present-day Americans such as you and me? Why were so many ordinary people willing to kill their Jewish neighbors under certain circumstances?

Ordinary people can be persuaded to do extraordinary and awful things. Given the right combination of ideology, authority, and gradual desensitization, all of us can become monsters, capable of destroying others with weapons ranging from words to gas chambers. It is a reality we must face and guard against, looking instead to God and trying to understand who he has called us to be.

THE TORTURE AND HUMILIATION OF THE KING

## They Led Him to Be Crucified

When the soldiers were done with Jesus, they put his clothes back on him and led him from the courtyard of Pilate's fortress toward the rocky hill on which he would be crucified. Its Latin name is Calvary—*Calvaria* means "skull"—and Golgotha is the Aramaic equivalent. The name "place of the skull" may have come from the presence of the skulls of criminals who had been put to death there—bodies were often left hanging, to be eaten by vultures or dogs—or it simply may have been that the hillside bore some resemblance to a skull. Today, visitors to Jerusalem are shown two possible locations for the hill. The site that stirs the imagination of most pilgrims is the less likely to be authentic. It is known as "Gordon's Calvary" after British general Charles Gordon, who suggested it after his visit to Palestine in 1882–83. It is a rock ledge that today overlooks a bus depot, but the formation resembles a skull. Nearby, Gordon discovered an ancient tomb that was quickly popularized as the possible site of Jesus' burial.

The more likely location of Golgotha, attested to by the early church, lies within the Church of the Holy Sepulchre. Visitors are taken up a set of stairs at the top of the hill to a chapel built over a rock formation approximately fifteen feet high. A glass case covers the top of the formation, and above that is an altar. It is believed that three holes would have been chiseled into the top of the formation to support the three crosses. When worshipers enter the room, many of them choose to go to the holiest place in the building, the altar table, and get on their knees, crawling underneath the altar to put their hands on the top of the rock where it is said Jesus was crucified. To approach it devotionally, to pause and reflect upon the story as they touch the very place, is a powerful experience. We can come to think of these stories we have read so often as myths or fairy tales. Being in such a place brings home powerfully that the events really happened, that God in human form walked and suffered and died here.

Calvary is about a third of a mile from where Pilate's palace stood. In Jesus' weakened state, the trip would have taken about thirty minutes. John tells us Jesus carried his own cross—likely just the crossbeam, as the vertical beam was probably left in place at the site of the executions. Making Jesus carry the cross on which he would be crucified gave the Romans one more opportunity to inflict humiliation and emotional pain on him. In contrast to John's account, Matthew, Mark, and Luke tell us Simon of Cyrene carried the cross. The two versions are not difficult to reconcile when we imagine Jesus carrying the beam for a few hundred yards until his dehydrated and physically weakened condition left him unable to go on.

Cyrene is a city in northern Libya, and Simon was probably a Jew visiting Jerusalem to celebrate the Passover when he was pressed into service. As he and Jesus neared Golgotha, or perhaps as they arrived at the site, someone offered Jesus a glass of wine mixed with myrrh (Mark 15:23). We believe myrrh served as an analgesic, something to deaden pain; so this may have been an act of compassion intended to help numb him to the worst part of the agony. This is the second time myrrh is mentioned in the Gospels (see Matthew 2:11); Jesus' mother, Mary, seeing this gesture, would have remembered the scene in which it was first mentioned: when myrrh was presented to her son just after his birth. It was a curious gift for the magi to bring, but now she understood it as prophetic.

Although Jesus had had nothing to eat or drink since the Last Supper, he refused the offer of a painkiller. It is as if he needed to say, "I will bear the full brunt of what I am about to do. I will not deaden the pain with drugs." His suffering was for the purpose of redemption. It was part of God's plan for him and the world, and he had determined he would experience it fully.

## The Power of Sacrificial Love

Christians believe, and Jesus clearly taught, that his suffering and death were the means of salvation for humanity. Through them, men and women would be offered forgiveness, redemption, and right standing with God. We looked at one theory of the Atonement in the last chapter: the substitutionary theory that states Jesus suffered and died in place of all who would trust in him as Savior. He died in our stead, taking upon himself the sin and punishment we deserve for violating the will of God. We will now consider another theory: the subjective or moral influence theory of the Atonement.

The subjective or moral influence theory of the Atonement maintains that the Atonement was not about changing God or making it possible for God to forgive us. It was, rather, about changing you and me. Jesus' suffering, death, and resurrection constitute a divine drama meant to communicate God's Word to humanity, to make clear to us our need for redemption and forgiveness, to show us the full extent of God's love and lead us to repentance. John's Gospel begins with a prologue in which he speaks of Jesus as God's Word. Jesus was God's vehicle for communicating with us, his Word made flesh. In Jesus, God's divine nature was united with human flesh to reveal his character, his love, and his will for humanity.

What was God trying to say in the suffering and death of Jesus? The events surrounding the last twenty-four hours of Jesus' life on Earth speak first of the brokenness of humanity. As we have seen already, each of the persons taking part in this tragedy is a reflection of that brokenness. The disciples fell asleep, then fled in fear as Jesus was arrested. Judas betrayed Jesus. Peter denied him. The Sanhedrin wished him dead. The crowds preferred a messiah preaching violence to a messiah preaching love. The governor wished to satisfy the crowd, and the soldiers took delight in torturing and dehumanizing an innocent man.

This story of what human beings did when God walked among us is an indictment of humanity. We are meant to find ourselves in that story and to be moved by its tragic end. We are meant to realize there is something deeply wrong with us, that we are broken and in need of forgiveness.

I have been to the National Holocaust Museum in Washington, DC, on several occasions. I have taken each of my daughters there to see the photos, the video footage, and the exhibits documenting the atrocities that occurred under Hitler's "final solution." The museum is a testament to the gross inhumanity of the Nazis; but it is also a witness to the complicity of millions of ordinary people in Europe who refused to resist this evil, including many leaders of the church. Even the United States, ultimately playing a key role in the defeat of Hitler, refused to receive larger numbers of Jewish immigrants from Europe at a time when the Nazis were implementing the "final solution." The Holocaust is an indictment not only upon the Nazis, but upon the entire human race.

My daughters and I walked in silence after our visits, deeply moved, disturbed, and convicted by what we had seen. That is the aim of the Holocaust Museum: to affect visitors so deeply that they leave committed to the proposition that this should never happen again.

In the same way, the subjective or moral influence theory of the Atonement suggests that the suffering and death of Christ are meant to affect deeply those who hear the story. Jesus' suffering and death are intended to be a mirror held up to our souls, a reminder of the jealousy, pettiness, self-centeredness, spiritual blindness, and darkness that lurk in all our souls. We are meant to read the Gospel accounts of the torture, humiliation, and crucifixion of Christ and say, "Never again!" or "God save us from ourselves. Lord have mercy upon us!" The accounts are meant to move us to repentance.

The brokenness of humanity is not the only word we are meant to hear in this story, however. We are also meant to see the love of the One who suffers for us, as well as his determination to save us from ourselves and from our sin. Jesus' suffering and death were not accidental. He chose the path he knew would end in his Passion. He faced the flagrum, the crown, and the cross with determination, silence, and dignity. He stood naked as if to say, "Do you see the extent of the Father's love yet? Do you understand that I have come so that you might finally hear of a love that is willing to suffer, yea, even to die, in order to win you over?"

Jesus demonstrates a love that refuses to give in to vengeance or to give up. He is determined to love the enemy in order to win freedom for them and restore them to the rightful relationship of beloved child and friend. Paul says in Romans 5:8, "God proves his love for us in that while we still were sinners Christ died for us"; and John 3:16 tells us, "For God so loved the world that he gave his only Son, so that everyone who believes in him may not perish but may have eternal life." The cross is the vehicle for demonstrating the full extent of God's love.

There is one more word we should hear in Jesus' suffering and death, and that concerns the nature of sacrificial love. He has set an example for us of a kind of love that alone has the power to save humanity from its self-destructive ways. Sacrificial love transforms enemies into friends, shames the guilty into repentance, and melts hearts of stone. The world is changed by true demonstrations of sacrificial love and by selfless acts of service.

In November of 2004, Tammy Duckworth, a reservist called up to fight in Iraq, was copilot of a Black Hawk helicopter struck by a rocket-propelled grenade that exploded at her feet, severing her legs and crushing her arm. By the time the chopper crash-landed, it appeared she was dead. The soldiers in the helicopter with Tammy knew the enemy would be on their way to the crash site and that if they were captured, they would likely be killed; but they refused to leave Tammy behind. They worked to extract her from the helicopter, then carried her through fields of six-foot-tall grasses at great personal risk in order to get her out. When they finally reached safety, they realized that although she had lost half her blood, she was, miraculously, alive. She recovered, was fitted for prosthetics, and is now fully mobile. Later, she was named director of the Illinois Department of Veterans Affairs. On February 3, 2009, Duckworth was nominated to be the Assistant Secretary of Public and Intergovernmental Affairs for the United States Department of Veterans Affairs. The United States Senate confirmed her for the position on April 22. Asked how she felt about the great risk her fellow soldiers took to save her, Major Duckworth said, "You have to get up every day and seek to live in such a way as to be worthy of that kind of effort and sacrifice."[5]

That is the power of sacrificial love, and that is exactly what the cross of Christ is meant to inspire us to do. We are to look at the cross of Jesus and say, "I have to strive to live in such a way as to be worthy of that sacrifice." We are meant to be changed by the Atonement and in turn to practice sacrificial love toward others. As each new follower of Jesus practices such love, the world will be changed and humanity transformed.

## The Legacy of Simon

Before we move on to the Crucifixion, I would like to draw your attention once more to Simon of Cyrene, who was pressed into service carrying the cross of Jesus. Was this visitor from

Libya simply a passer-by in the wrong place at the wrong time, or had he been watching Jesus suffer unjustly? Is it possible he was actually a follower of Jesus who risked his own life in order to help?

We cannot know if Simon was a follower of Jesus before this encounter, but Mark gives us an intriguing hint that from this time forward he did follow Jesus and that the experience of carrying the cross of Christ affected him deeply. Mark 15:21 tells us, "They compelled a passer-by, who was coming in from the country, to carry his cross; it was Simon of Cyrene, the father of Alexander and Rufus." The fact that Mark mentions the names of Simon's sons while Luke and Matthew do not would indicate that the people to whom Mark was writing his Gospel—the Christians in Rome approximately thirty-six years later—knew who Alexander and Rufus were. By this time, no doubt, Simon was dead. In Romans 16:13, Paul, writing to the Christians in Rome just a few years before Mark composed his Gospel, said, "Greet Rufus, chosen in the Lord; and greet his mother— a mother to me also." It seems likely this Rufus was the son of Simon. He was by then a leader in the church, "chosen in the Lord"; and his mother had been especially close to Paul. Simon was apparently so moved by the experience of suffering next to Jesus, of carrying his cross and then watching him be crucified, that he became the first believer transformed by the moral influence of the Atonement. His heart was moved by Jesus' suffering, and he decided to follow him. Simon's wife and children became followers of Jesus as well.

Where do you see yourself in the portion of the story we have considered in this chapter? Do you recognize yourself in the soldiers? They knelt before Jesus and said, "Hail, king of the Jews!" but in their hearts they mocked him. These were men who loved power, who enjoyed inflicting pain on others, and who were ultimately blind. I asked a friend, "Have you ever mocked Jesus by your words or actions?" and he replied, "When do I not mock him? I feel like most of my life I struggle with mocking Jesus, with saying one thing about him when I'm in church but then often mocking him with my thoughts and actions the rest of the week. I don't live as though he is my King." Do you ever hail Jesus as King on Sunday and mock him by your words and deeds on Monday?

Yet we might also recognize ourselves in Simon. He saw Jesus suffer and was so moved that he became a follower; and decades later, after he was gone, his wife and sons continued to serve the Lord. That is the kind of transformation we each might seek as we look at the suffering and death of Christ.

---

[1] From *Nicene and Post-Nicene Fathers, Second Series* (Hendrickson Publishers, 1999); Vol. 1, page 189.

[2] From Wikipedia; see http://en.wikipedia.org/wiki/Stanford_prison_experiment. (March 30, 2006)

[3] See Transforming People Into Perpetrators of Evil, by Philip Zimbardo; http://www.sonoma.edu/users/g/goodman/zimbardo.htm. (June 2009)

[4] See Transforming People Into Perpetrators of Evil, by Philip Zimbardo.

[5] From NPR, Morning Edition; see http://www.npr.org/templates/story/story.php?storyId=5308074. (March 29, 2006)

# 6. The Crucifixion

*It was nine o'clock in the morning when they crucified him. The inscription of the charge against him read, "The King of the Jews." And with him they crucified two bandits, one on his right and one on his left. Those who passed by derided him, shaking their heads and saying, "Aha! You who would destroy the temple and build it in three days, save yourself, and come down from the cross!" In the same way the chief priests, along with the scribes, were also mocking him among themselves and saying, "He saved others; he cannot save himself. Let the Messiah, the King of Israel, come down from the cross now, so that we may see and believe." Those who were crucified with him also taunted him.*

*When it was noon, darkness came over the whole land until three in the afternoon. At three o'clock Jesus cried out with a loud voice, "Eloi, Eloi, lema sabachthani?" which means, "My God, my God, why have you forsaken me?" When some of the bystanders heard it, they said, "Listen, he is calling for Elijah." And someone ran, filled a sponge with sour wine, put it on a stick, and gave it to him to drink, saying, "Wait, let us see whether Elijah will come to take him down." Then Jesus gave a loud cry and breathed his last. And the curtain of the temple was torn in two, from top to bottom. Now when the centurion, who stood facing him, saw that in this way he breathed his last, he said, "Truly this man was God's Son!"*

(MARK 15:25-39)

## Friday
### 9:00 AM–3:00 PM
### GOLGOTHA, OUTSIDE THE WALLS OF JERUSALEM

### "The Most Pitiable of Deaths"

WE COME NOW to the cross.

The Romans, as we have seen, practiced crucifixion as a means of striking fear in the hearts of the people; and they did so for eight hundred years. It was a terrifying death, and those who witnessed it were not inclined thereafter to violate Roman law. Seneca said that if you knew there was a likelihood you would be arrested and crucified, it was better to commit suicide.[1] Cicero called crucifixion the "extreme and ultimate punishment of slaves" and the "cruelest and most disgusting penalty."[2] Josephus called it "the most pitiable of deaths."[3]

Crucifixion was an extremely effective crime deterrent, since crucifixions took place along the main thoroughfares where people would see them. The vertical beam of the cross was left in place at the site. The criminal, after he was flogged, carried the crossbeam, which could weigh a hundred pounds. Victims were typically left hanging, or their bodies were taken down and left on the ground near the cross until the animals were finished with them. Some of the bodies were placed on a trash heap, and bones simply may have been scattered unless loved ones claimed them. There was ordinarily no allowance by the Romans for people to come and take the bodies. In Jerusalem, however, people could bury their dead after crucifixion.

The goal of crucifixion was to inflict the maximum agony for the longest possible time. Victims could hang on the cross for days before they finally died. Depending on what was convenient for the Romans, the victim's arms could be nailed to the cross at the wrists, which were considered part of the hands; or the arms

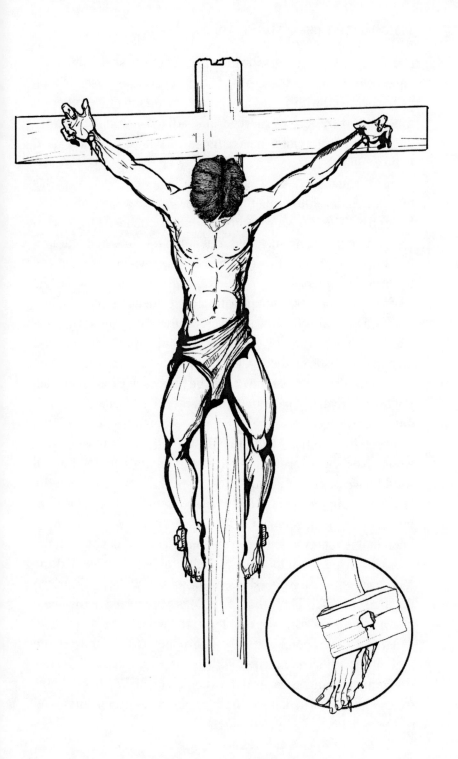

could be tied to the cross with ropes. The feet seem always to have been nailed to the cross. The crucifixion of Jesus is typically portrayed with Jesus' feet being one on top of the other on the front of the cross, pierced and affixed to the wood with one nail. Recent studies have suggested this picture may need to be modified.

In 1968, just outside Jerusalem, an ossuary or "bone box" was found, belonging to a man of about twenty-seven identified as Yehonnan. The human remains inside were believed to be from the first century and included a heel bone with a nail still protruding through it and wrist bones bearing evidence of damage from rope that had apparently cut through the skin. This was the first set of bones ever found with clear evidence of crucifixion. The find has caused some scholars to revise their image of crucifixion. They believe the victim's legs would have been bent and turned to the side so the ankles were one behind the other at the front of the cross, where they could be pierced with one long nail. Further study has challenged even this revised picture. The nail found in the heel bone of Yehonnan was about five inches long. Between the nail head and the bone are fragments of wood that would have been pressed against the victim's foot—the nail would have pierced the wood first, then the bone, and then the cross, holding the victim's foot in place. Looking more closely at this arrangement, scholars determined the nail would not have been long enough to have pierced both feet and penetrated the cross. This led them to suggest the victim would have had the feet pressed against the sides of the cross, with a nail driven through each. It is likely that Jesus' legs were nailed in this manner; we know his arms were nailed at the wrists rather than tied.

The legs of Yehonnan had been broken, as John tells us the legs of the thieves crucified with Jesus were. It was a means the Romans sometimes used to expedite death. We do not know exactly how it worked; it may have caused a blood clot, increased the shock or stress to the system, or made it harder to rise up and breathe.

It is common to imagine the crucified Jesus at a considerable height off the ground, but it is now believed most crosses were no more than nine feet tall. Allowing room at the top of the cross for the sign that was affixed detailing the victim's crime, it is likely that the feet of the victim were at most three feet off the ground. Jesus hung on the cross just two to three feet above his mother, the disciple John, the soldiers, and those who hurled insults at him. He could look into their eyes, and they could look into his. They were much closer than most imagine, something you can visualize by standing atop a chair beside someone standing at ground level—this was the proximity of Jesus to the people at the foot of the cross.

Some believe asphyxiation was a common cause of death among those crucified. Hanging on a cross, it was very difficult to exhale without raising oneself up. The longer one hung on the cross and the more exhausted one became, the more difficult it was to exhale. Breathing became more and more shallow, so that crucifixion became a slow death by asphyxiation. Others believe a buildup of fluid around the heart caused congestive heart failure. A loss of fluids and subsequent dehydration is also seen as a possible cause of death, as is hypovolemic shock (closely tied to dehydration and loss of blood and producing, among other symptoms, increased agitation and anxiety in the victim). Others see these factors acting in combination. What we know for certain is that this was an extremely effective way to torture someone for a great length of time. Jesus, bloodied and naked, hung that way for six hours.

## The Atonement as Sacrifice

We understand why the Jewish leaders, the crowd, and the Romans wanted to crucify Jesus; but why did Jesus seem to face this death so willingly, to embrace it as a part of his mission? And why did God send Jesus, knowing this would happen?

Christians point to Jesus' death on the cross as that historical event in which God was at work bringing about the salvation of the world. Paul writes in Romans 5:6-11:

> For while we were still weak, at the right time Christ died for the ungodly. Indeed, rarely will anyone die for a righteous person— though perhaps for a good person someone might actually dare to die. But God proves his love for us in that while we still were sinners Christ died for us. Much more surely then, now that we have been justified by his blood, will we be saved through him from the wrath of God. For if while we were enemies, we were reconciled to God through the death of his Son, much more surely, having been reconciled, will we be saved by his life. But more than that, we even boast in God through our Lord Jesus Christ, through whom we have now received reconciliation.

In this passage and in the rest of Romans 5, Paul offers us several ways of thinking about how Jesus' death on the cross saves us. The Book of Hebrews gives us another, the rest of the Epistles another, the Gospels yet another. There are a variety of theories of the Atonement. We have looked at two of them so far, considering the substitutionary theory of the Atonement, in which Jesus is seen as taking our place, receiving the punishment humanity deserves for sin, and the subjective or moral influence theory of the Atonement, in which Jesus' suffering and death demonstrate the depth of human sin and the breadth of God's love in a way meant to move us to repentance and a deep desire to follow God. Now we will consider what I will call the sacrificial offering theory of the Atonement.

As early as Genesis 4, we see human beings bringing sacrificial offerings to God. Grain, animal, wine, oil, and monetary offerings were presented to God by mortals as expressions of gratitude, devotion, love, and worship. In bringing those offerings, believers were united with God. When LaVon and I give our tithes and offerings to God, we do so not simply to meet the church's budget or to win God's favor. Even though our offerings are an expression of our gratitude to God, they represent something far more than that. We give them as an expression of our desire to belong wholly to God, to honor and love him and put him first in our lives. Giving our tithes and offerings is an act of worship for us. In our ordinary lives, we often give gifts that express our appreciation, love, and devotion to another.

Sacrificial offerings are also a part of the process of expressing sorrow and repentance. When we hurt others, we are alienated from them until we have acknowledged our transgression, asked for forgiveness, and done what we can to make things right. When you get in a fight with your spouse and then realize you were in the wrong, what do you do? You might leave him a note the next day and look for ways to bless him as an expression of your regret and of your desire to be in right relationship with him. You might bring her flowers and tell her how sorry you are. In any case, through such expressions you atone for your sins. It is not that you cannot be forgiven without making such a gesture. In fact, we routinely receive forgiveness without offering a gift to the one we have hurt. But there are moments when the giving of a token to express one's regret makes a difference.

Likewise, in our relationship with God there is a need to acknowledge our sin, to repent of it, and to seek to make things right. In the Old Testament, God made provision for the people to make amends and be restored to a right relationship with him. They could do this by making sin offerings or guilt offerings. If you had violated God's will, you brought a special offering to the Lord to say, "I'm sorry for what I did, oh God. Please accept this offering as an expression of my remorse and my repentance. Forgive me and make me clean again." With such an offering, people could feel relieved of guilt and restored to a right relationship with God; so this was a regular part of worship.

Then, once a year, on the Day of Atonement—Yom Kippur—there were special sacrifices. Even before there was a temple, there was a tent in which the people met; and within the tent was the throne room of God. It was surrounded by a curtain; and inside was the ark of the covenant, the throne of God. Once a year the high priest was to offer a bull as a sacrifice for his own sins and the sins of his family. He was to bathe, and then he and he alone would go inside the curtain. He would offer a goat as a sacrifice to God on behalf of the people, saying, "God, with this goat's blood I offer this sacrifice, a living creature dying that you might forgive these people. I come on their behalf, pleading with you to forgive their sins and remember the sins no more." It was a powerful drama demonstrating the seriousness of sin and the willingness of God to forgive. This sacrifice, along with a host of guilt offerings, was made not to turn away God's wrath, but to express the people's repentance and their desire to be reconciled to God.

Once the goat was offered for the sins of the people, the priest would take a second goat and figuratively place the sins of the people upon it. This was the scapegoat, which was taken away from the dwellings and sent out into the wilderness. The people came to understand that, just as that goat had gone away, never to be seen again, their sins had been carried away.

In the sacrificial offering theory of the Atonement, we view the Crucifixion through the lens of the Old Testament's sacrificial system. In his death, Jesus acted as the high priest representing all of humanity. Throughout the Gospels, Jesus refers to himself as the Son of Man, a title pointing to his role as "representative human being." He was God in the flesh, revealing God to us; but he was also fully human, representing a new humanity that reflected what we were meant to be as human beings. In this capacity, he became our priest and intercessor with God. He offered a sacrifice to God to atone for humanity's sin, to reconcile us with the Father. He offered not a goat or a bull, but himself as the Son of Man and as our high priest. In essence, he said, "Father, for these creatures, so small, so broken, so easily lured into hurting one another, for these men and women who do evil to one another and turn their backs on you—for them I offer myself to you to atone for their sins."

The Scriptures speak of God's Son, Jesus, sitting at the right hand of the Father. I will leave it to others to explain the precise nature of the Trinity, but here I would simply say that Jesus Christ is ever with the Father. In the Father's presence, Christ's self-giving sacrifice is never forgotten. His wounds are a perpetual reminder of the price he was willing to pay to restore humanity to a right relationship with God. His magnanimous act—his suffering and death on behalf of humanity—served as an atoning sacrifice for all people; and the Father, by virtue of the Son's love and self-giving, bestows grace and mercy upon all who claim the Son as their high priest and Savior. God the Father offers forgiveness and grace to us not because of our own merit, but because his dearly loved Son suffered and died on behalf of the human race.

Again, this view of the Atonement suggests that Jesus' suffering and death on the cross represent Jesus' self-giving, his offering on our behalf. He gave himself wholly to God as an offering on our behalf, to win God's mercy for us. Jesus is always with the Father, and hence he is continually making intercession on our behalf. He is a perpetual offering for humanity. And his sacrifice is one the Father could never set aside or ignore.

Years ago, while on a family vacation, my younger daughter took all the spending money she had for the entire trip and used it to buy me a ball cap for my birthday. She was so excited to give me the cap. When she gave it to me and I realized she had given up all her spending money to buy it, I was moved to tears. The hat was an expression of her love, an expression that included real sacrifice. My daughter is now grown; but I still treasure that dirty, stained, and well-worn cap. I never look at it without smiling and remembering how much my daughter loves me. And this is just a ball cap. In Jesus' sacrificial offering to the Father, he gave himself to win our forgiveness and God's mercy. His nail-scarred hands are a perpetual reminder to the Father of Christ's sacrifice for us. His offering has won God's favor.

With this view of the Atonement, we have considered three different ways of making sense of Jesus' suffering and death and how they bring salvation to humankind. In the final chapter of this book, when we focus on Easter, we will consider one additional theory of the Atonement. The fact that the meaning of Jesus' suffering and death is open to different interpretations and that even the New Testament authors appear to have different ways of making sense of it seems to indicate that God may well have intended it this way. The Gospel writers themselves were clear that the suffering and death of Christ were central to God's saving work in him, but they did not attempt to spell out precisely how Christ's suffering brings about the salvation of humanity.

In many ways, the suffering and death of Christ seem meant by God to function like a masterpiece of art—they speak in different ways to different people at different times in their lives. In my own life, it has been just that way. At moments when I have been most ashamed of something I have done, I have felt Christ to be my substitute and have been comforted by the punishment he bore on my behalf. At other times, I have seen in his suffering and death the brokenness in my own life; and I have been amazed by the love of God that refuses to give up on me. Christ's cross has beckoned me at times to give myself fully and selflessly to others and to God's work. At still other times I picture Jesus offering himself to God on my behalf, and I am moved to gratitude and love.

However you understand the death of Jesus, the fact of its atoning work in restoring us to right relationship with God is made clear by one small detail in the accounts of the Crucifixion found in Matthew, Mark, and Luke. Mark writes, "Then Jesus gave a loud cry and breathed his last. And the curtain of the temple was torn in two, from top to bottom" (Mark 15:37-38). This curtain was the one separating the Holy of Holies—the throne room of God—from the rest of the Temple. It was the one behind which the high priest alone could go, and then only once a year, to atone for the sins of the people. By telling us the curtain was torn asunder when Christ died, the Gospel writers are pointing to the idea that in his death Jesus atoned for our sins as our high priest. He tore down the curtain that separated humanity from God. He offered us, by his death, reconciliation and atonement with God.

## The Last Words of Jesus

Before leaving the Crucifixion, let's give special attention to the dying words of Jesus. The last words of any man or woman carry special weight. I have been with people when they were dying, have watched them move their lips with what little strength they had to say one last "I love you" or to join me one final time in saying the Lord's Prayer. Each of the Gospels records a phrase or two that Jesus spoke from the cross. He hung there for six hours and probably said far more than this, but these were the words people remembered. They have special meaning, and each deserves a chapter of its own; but here we will consider only briefly each of these final statements of Jesus to see what it teaches us about him. I will deal with them in the order I imagine they were spoken.

### "Here is your mother" (John 19:27).

John tells us Jesus looked down from the cross to see his mother standing nearby. I imagine her weeping there throughout the six-hour ordeal. As far as we know, only one of the twelve apostles was there at the foot of the cross: "the disciple whom Jesus loved," usually identified as John himself. While Jesus suffered on the cross, naked and in pain, he was not thinking of himself but of his mother, who was standing close enough that he could look her in the eyes. He was concerned for her well-being after his death. This is a beautiful scene that demonstrates both Jesus' humanity and the depth of love he had for his mother and for the disciple into whose care he entrusted her.

**"Father, forgive them; for they do not know what they are doing" (Luke 23:34).**

These are the most magnificent and majestic words ever uttered by a dying man. They were echoed by Stephen in Acts 7:60 as he was martyred for his faith. Jesus looked from the cross at the soldiers casting lots for his clothing, at the priests pointing to him with disgust, at the crowd hurling their insults, at the thieves on his left and right mocking him. At this moment the evil that resides in human beings was seen at its apex. As God, Jesus could have called for legions of angels to bring vengeance on them all. Instead, he pulled himself up and with all his strength offered a prayer on behalf of those who mocked and crucified him. "Father, forgive them," he prayed; "for they do not know what they are doing." What was on his heart at that moment was the fact that we are blind, stupid, pitiable creatures; and he was crying out on the cross for mercy for us.

How was this possible? Here we see once again Jesus' clarity of mission. His death was purposeful. Even as his enemies were mocking him and subjecting him to the most torturous of all deaths, Jesus was pleading for our forgiveness. This was Jesus our High Priest making intercession for us. He wished even his torturers to be forgiven. Imagine the impact of his words on the crowd. Do you think that for at least an instant they were silenced and put to shame? I am guessing some of them would never forget the moment when they heard Jesus speak these words.

### "Today you will be with me in Paradise" (Luke 23:43).

Two thieves crucified by the Romans hung on crosses next to Jesus, one on either side. They were dying terrible deaths, and yet one of them joined the crowd in mocking the man dying between them. But as Jesus prayed for the very people crucifying and mocking him, one of the thieves listened and was both amazed and ashamed. Somehow the blinders came off, and he was able to see that this was no ordinary criminal. He understood something of the essence of Jesus. The other thief continued to insult Jesus; but this one said, "Stop. Don't you see? We deserve to die. This man doesn't. He is innocent" (paraphrase of Luke 23:40-41). He turned to Jesus and said, "Remember me when you come into your kingdom" (Luke 23:42); and Jesus raised himself up yet again and said, "Today you will be with me in Paradise" (Luke 23:43). I love this. Jesus, hanging on the cross, was still seeking to save those who were lost. This man did not understand theology. He did not know Scripture. He had not recited a creed. He had not joined a church or been baptized. He had not had the chance to do anything righteous or to clean up his life. He was hanging on the cross for his crimes when, at some very simple level, he caught the vision of Jesus' kingdom and asked if he might become part of it; and that was enough. "Now that I see who you are," he was saying, in effect, "I'd like to follow you." For us, as for the thief on the cross, this is a sufficient starting point. We can look to the Lord and say, "Jesus, remember me when you come into your kingdom. I want to follow you. Help me to do that."

Jesus' detractors called him "a friend of tax collectors and sinners" (Matthew 11:19; Luke 7:34). He told his disciples just a week before his death that "the Son of Man came to seek out and to save the lost" (Luke 19:10). He spent much of his public life with outcasts, tax collectors, and prostitutes. He died on a cross between two thieves. One of these thieves, though hanging just inches from the Son of God, was still blinded by sin. But the other man saw in Jesus, hanging there by his side on the cross, a glimpse of glory and of the love of God and joined himself to Jesus. Jesus' words to this man spoke volumes about the nature of God's mercy and of salvation.

### "My God, my God, why have you forsaken me?" (Matthew 27:46; Mark 15:34; see Psalm 22:1).

Hour after interminable hour, Jesus hung in agony on the cross; and during that time, God his Father was silent. As Jesus spoke, we hear not hope, but defeat. Matthew and Mark both recorded these words; and we learn that some of those standing by the cross were confused by them, while others heard them clearly and interpreted them as being the words of a man feeling complete despair.

Jesus cried out, "My God, my God, why have you forsaken me?"

These are unsettling words to some. Did Jesus truly feel forsaken by God at that moment? Would God forsake his Son?

Some have explained Jesus' words by suggesting that at that moment God placed upon him the sins of the world and then was forced to turn away because a holy God cannot look upon sin. I find this a wholly inadequate explanation—it takes too literal a view of Jesus bearing the sins of humanity on the cross. What exactly would God have placed on Jesus? What would it have looked like? More importantly, would the Father really have looked away from his Son at the moment of Jesus' greatest saving act? This seems unthinkable. I believe it more likely that God never removed his gaze from Jesus during those hours on the cross. God the Father suffered with the Son.

If Jesus' words were not prompted by the Father's turning away from him, why did he offer what is sometimes called the "cry of dereliction"? Was God, in fact, derelict?

What we are seeing in the words of Jesus is his humanity. He was experiencing what most of us face to a lesser degree in our lives: a moment when the silence of God is so deafening that we feel forsaken by him. Pain and doubt creep in and block out any sense of God's presence. We do not see how God can make the situation turn out for good. God seems far away, and our prayers appear to go unanswered. The joy of God's presence has disappeared. How grateful I am that Jesus knows what it is to pray, "Let this cup pass from me" (Matthew 26:39); but how much more grateful I am that he came to a place where he felt compelled to cry out, "My God, my God, why have you forsaken me?" He knows what you and I feel at our times of despair because he experienced such despair himself. The fact that even Jesus felt such despair offers us some consolation when we go through it. And we find hope as we remember that Jesus ultimately experienced deliverance and that though he felt forsaken, he was not.

It is important to note that in crying out these words, Jesus was quoting Psalm 22:1. This is a reminder of the importance of the psalms in Jesus' own prayer life; and this is also a reminder that the psalmist, too, felt forsaken by God. It is valuable to read the whole of Psalm 22, and I would encourage you to do so. Again and again it mirrors the experience of Jesus at his crucifixion. In fact, Jesus' use of these words from the psalm was likely also meant to prompt his disciples to read it. It is easy to see why this psalm came to mind for Jesus, but it is also worth noting that the psalm ends on a note of triumph and hope. In verse 24 we read that God

> Did not despise or abhor
> the affliction of the afflicted;

> he did not hide his face from me,
> but heard when I cried to him.

The psalm continues by noting that

> To him, indeed, shall all who sleep in the earth bow down;
> before him shall bow all who go down to the dust,
> and I shall live for him.
> Posterity will serve him;
> future generations will be told about the LORD,
> and proclaim his deliverance to a people yet unborn,
> saying that he has done it. (Psalm 22:29-31)

Like the writers of the psalms, Jesus was expressing true despair and feelings of abandonment; yet his quotation of Psalm 22 points to the same faith the psalmist had. Though he felt God had forsaken him, he still trusted that God would ultimately deliver him.

## "I am thirsty" (John 19:28).

The hours crept by, and the pain and agony continued to take their toll. Jesus became dehydrated by the loss of blood and sweat. He had had nothing to eat or drink since the Last Supper the night before. Life ebbed from him. His mouth was parched. John records him saying, "I am thirsty."

In John's Gospel, everything is written at two levels; and true to form, Jesus' words here have both a surface meaning and a deeper one. He was a human being, dehydrated, painfully thirsty, his tongue sticking to the roof of his mouth; but we are meant to remember another moment when Jesus was thirsty. In John 4, as Jesus walked through Samaria, he came to a well where he met a local woman. "Give me a drink," he said to her (John 4:7). "The Samaritan woman said to him, 'How is it that you, a Jew, ask a drink of me, a woman of Samaria?' (Jews do not share things in common with Samaritans.) Jesus answered her, 'If you knew the gift of God, and who it is that is saying to you, "Give me a drink," you would have asked him, and he would have given you living water.... Those who drink of the water that I will give them will never be thirsty. The water that I will give will become in them a spring of water gushing up to eternal life.'" (John 4:9-10, 14). Jesus' words, "I am thirsty," are meant to pierce the heart of the reader with grief. The Source of living water by which we might never thirst again was himself thirsty, the eternal spring was drying up, and his life was ebbing away.

John, like the other Gospels, tells us someone near the cross offered Jesus a drink of sour wine; but only John tells us this person placed a sponge dipped in wine on a hyssop branch and held it to Jesus' lips. Once again we find John using a small detail to point to something of deeper significance. God had commanded that hyssop branches be used to sprinkle the blood of the Passover lamb above the doors of the dwellings of the Israelites when the firstborn of the Egyptians were killed (Exodus 12:22). It was hyssop wrapped in yarn that was used to sprinkle blood and water upon the lepers (Leviticus 14) and on the ceremonially unclean (Numbers 19) so that they might be made clean again. When David offered his prayer of confession in Psalm 51, he cried out to God, "Purge me with hyssop, and I shall be clean" (verse 7); and the writer of Hebrews notes that after Moses gave the people the commandments, "he took the blood of calves and goats, with water and scarlet wool and hyssop, and sprinkled both the scroll itself and all the people, saying, 'This is the blood of the covenant that God has ordained for you.'" (Hebrews 9:19-20). Though John does not include Jesus' words at the Last Supper, "This is my blood of the covenant, which is poured out for many for the forgiveness of sins" (Matthew 26:28), he intends the reader to understand and recall this idea when he includes the detail of the hyssop branch used to offer wine to satisfy Jesus' thirst.

### "Father, into your hands I commend my spirit" (Luke 23:46).

Like Psalm 22, nearly all the lament psalms—those that complain because God seems to be nowhere near—end with an affirmation of faith. The very act of praying a complaint psalm is an affirmation of faith. When darkness seems to prevail in your life, it takes faith even to talk to God and complain to him! The last words of Jesus from the cross recorded in the Gospel of Luke reflect Jesus' absolute trust in God: "Father, into your hands I commend my spirit." This is also a model of prayer for all of us when we are afraid, when we are sick, when we face our own death. This prayer says, "I commit myself to you, O God. In my living and in my dying, in the good times and in the bad, whatever I am and have, I place in your hands, O God, for your safekeeping."

### "It is finished" (John 19:30).

Then, finally, Jesus spoke these words, which were a cry not of dereliction, but of victory: "It is finished." There is determination in these words. What Jesus came to do, he had now completed. A plan was fulfilled. A salvation was made possible, a love shown. He had taken our place. He had demonstrated both humanity's brokenness and God's love. He had offered himself fully to God as a sacrifice on behalf of humanity. As he died, it was finished. With these words, the noblest person who ever walked the face of this planet, God in the flesh, breathed his last.

### Seeing Yourself in the Story

Before leaving this scene, I invite you to consider the soldiers present at the foot of the cross. Luke and John tell us some of them were busy casting lots for Jesus' clothing. The soldiers saw Jesus dying but did not understand what was really happening. They were taking what their limited perspective saw as being of value—his clothing—while missing the infinite value of the eternal life Jesus was offering at that moment. But Mark tells us that one soldier "stood facing him," heard his final words, and saw how he took his last breath. This soldier, having seen all that took place during those six hours at the Crucifixion, uttered these words: "Truly this man was God's Son!" (Mark 15:39).

I invite you to find yourself in this story. Will you be like the soldiers who cast lots for Jesus' clothing, who missed the power and mystery and wonder of the cross and whose only interest was in a few rags of clothing? Will you finish this book and go back to caring primarily about the things of the world—clothes, cars, vacations, status? Or will you be like the soldier who, having seen all these events that took place in the last hours of Jesus' life, was moved to say, "Truly this man was God's Son"?

---

[1] From *Seneca's Epistles*, Volume 111; see http://www.stoics.com/seneca_epistles_book_3html. (April 4, 2006)

[2] From *Bible History On Line*; see http://www.bible-history.com/past/flagrum.html. (April 4, 2006)

[3] From *Bible History On Line*; see http://www.bible-history.com/past/flagrum.html. (April 4, 2006)

# 7. Christ the Victor

*When the sabbath was over, Mary Magdalene, and Mary the mother of James, and Salome bought spices, so that they might go and anoint him. And very early on the first day of the week, when the sun had risen, they went to the tomb. They had been saying to one another, "Who will roll away the stone for us from the entrance to the tomb?" When they looked up, they saw that the stone, which was very large, had already been rolled back. As they entered the tomb, they saw a young man, dressed in a white robe, sitting on the right side; and they were alarmed. But he said to them, "Do not be alarmed; you are looking for Jesus of Nazareth, who was crucified. He has been raised; he is not here." (MARK 16:1-6)*

## Friday
### 6:00 AM
### AN EMPTY TOMB NEAR JERUSALEM

### The First Day

WITH THE DEATH of Jesus on Calvary, we witness, amid the cacophony of soldiers and criminals, gawkers and passers-by, what looks like the final triumph of evil. All the ugliness and violence we can imagine was embodied in the events that had as their climax the six hours during which God in human form hung on a cross on a hillside outside the gates of Jerusalem.

We cannot really appreciate Easter until we have been to the cross. The power of this day lies beyond our comprehension until we have journeyed through hell itself, immersed in the darkest of places. It is only once we have seen the full extent of evil on display there and witnessed the apparent victory of death that we can begin to appreciate the triumph that is Easter.

Jesus died at about three o'clock on Friday afternoon. The Jewish sabbath would begin at sunset three hours later (Jewish days end and begin at sunset.); and this, the Passover sabbath, was particularly important. The Jewish authorities did not want the bodies of the crucified still hanging on their crosses, so they petitioned Pilate to hasten their deaths by breaking their legs. The soldiers did so with the thieves; but as they came to Jesus, they found he had already breathed his last.

Approximately two hours before sunset, Jesus and the two thieves were taken down from their crosses. Since Jewish regulations did not permit burial on the sabbath, there was only a short window of time in which to make arrangements and prepare Jesus' body for burial. His disciples had scattered; but all four Gospels tell us that one of his followers, Joseph of Arimathea, was courageous enough to petition Pilate for permission to bury Jesus and that Pilate granted his request.

Mark tells us Joseph was a "respected member of the council" (Mark 15:43)—that is, of the Sanhedrin that had condemned Jesus to death. Matthew tells us he was a "rich man" and "a disciple of Jesus" (Matthew 27:57). Luke describes him as "a good and righteous man . . . who, though a member of the council, had not agreed to their plan and action" (Luke 23:50-51). John tells us he was "a disciple of Jesus, though a secret one because of his fear of the Jews" (John 19:38). The composite picture they paint dispels the notion that only the poor, the uneducated, and "sinners" were followers of Jesus; and it shows us that not all the Jewish religious leaders sought Jesus' death.

Joseph's fear of identifying himself publicly as one of Jesus' disciples (as depicted in the Gospel of John) makes him not unlike a number of respected members of society I have known. They fear what others might think of them if they were to identify themselves as persons who take their faith seriously. What might have been the cost to Joseph, a respected and wealthy member of Jewish society, had he identified himself as one of Jesus' disciples? If he had done so regardless, publicly declaring his support for Jesus, how might he have influenced others? How might things have turned out differently?

In what ways do you identify with Joseph? Are you ever a "secret disciple" for fear of what others will think?

Joseph's fear apparently left him when Jesus died, and he hurried to prepare the body for burial. John tells us he was joined by another secret disciple of Jesus: Nicodemus (John 19:39), who was also a "leader of the Jews" (John 3:1). Nicodemus brought with him approximately one hundred pounds of myrrh and aloes; and the two men, with no time for full burial preparations (which would have taken several hours), quickly cleaned Jesus' body and wrapped it in a linen shroud. Matthew (27:60) tells us Joseph placed Jesus "in his own new tomb," freshly "hewn in the rock" in what John (19:41) describes as a garden area near the site of Jesus' crucifixion. Joseph then had a large stone rolled in front of the entrance.

If we combine the Gospel accounts, the total number of people in attendance at Jesus' interment was four. Joseph, Nicodemus, and two of the women who followed Jesus—Mary Magdalene and another Mary—were the only ones who dared to come. The apostles were behind locked doors, terrified they might be arrested and subject to the fate that had befallen their Lord.

With sunset came the Passover sabbath; and while others cel-ebrated, those who knew and loved Jesus were in shock, trau-matized by what they had witnessed.

## The Second Day

We have no record of what occurred that Friday night follow-ing the Crucifixion and burial or throughout the day on Satur-day. We are left to imagine and interpolate based upon what we read in the Gospels. Matthew (27:62-66) tells us Pilate set a guard at the tomb because, according to the Pharisees, Jesus had said something about rising from the dead. They worried that the dis-ciples might take Jesus' body and claim he had indeed risen. Luke (23:56b) says simply that "on the sabbath they rested according to the commandment." John (20:19) gives us the detail that on Sunday the disciples were in a house with the doors locked for fear of being arrested, and it seems likely they had been there since Friday night. Some have speculated that this was the same "upper room" where Jesus celebrated the Passover with them on Thursday night and where the disciples would meet on the Day of Pentecost when the Spirit descended upon them.

It would be difficult to overstate the depths to which the disci-ples' spirits must have fallen. Fear that they could face Jesus' fate was just part of it. There was also the guilt. They knew Judas was not the only one who had betrayed him. Peter could not shake the moment when his eyes met Jesus' in the courtyard of the high priest after his denial that he even knew him (Luke 22:54-62). The rest had fled in Jesus' hour of need. Only John stood near the cross; the others watched from a distance. None had shown up for Jesus' burial. They felt themselves to be cowards.

Guilt and fear were not all they carried in their hearts that day, however. They had left everything to follow Jesus. They believed that he was the Messiah who would restore Israel. They believed that God was with him in powerful ways and that he had the "words of life." In him they had seen goodness personified. He had shown them love, mercy, and grace. Now the unthinkable had happened. Evil, perpetrated by those who claimed to be righteous, had defeated goodness. Rome's soldiers had defeated God's Messiah. Their King was gone. Their hopes and dreams, even their faith, had been crucified with him; and they must have sunk into utter despair.

As I think of the disciples on this second day after Jesus' death, I am reminded of the many times I have sat with families following the death of a young person; of sitting in a hospital waiting room with two dozen teenagers as their friend's life support was removed; of silence sprinkled with intermittent sobs as I sat in the home of the family of a young woman who was murdered. Now and then there are attempts at "normalcy" in times such as these, but nothing can lift the pall of death or the feeling in the heart when the weight of grief presses down upon it.

This is the second day—the day *after*. It is a day we all will know. It is the day after the diagnosis of terminal cancer; the day after a spouse walks out, leaving your life, your future, your hopes, and your heart in tatters. It is the day after the lawsuit is filed against you and the day after the verdict. It is the day after 9/11, the day the news is still sinking in and you realize your life will change forever. It is the day when the world seems so dark that hope is nowhere to be found.

Yet even on this day, with despair an unseen yet palpable presence, occasionally one of the disciples must have spoken up and said, "What was it he said about Jonah being in the belly of the whale for three days?" The others would dismiss the comment. Then, a second disciple would speak up. "Didn't he say something about destroying the Temple and in three days it would be rebuilt? Could he have been talking about being restored to life?"

To which the others would reply, "No, that's not what he meant." Still another would say, "I could swear he did say that the Son of Man would be put to death, but he would rise again." These words of Jesus had not been understood when he uttered them, and even now they seemed absurd. Four people had seen his tortured body placed in the tomb. It was unfathomable that he would return.

## "He Descended Into Hell"

What was the spirit of Jesus doing on this second day? Did he rest on the sabbath as his body lay in the tomb; or did he, as affirmed in one version of the Apostle's Creed, descend "into hell"? This doctrine, known in medieval English as the "harrowing of hell," held that at his death Jesus descended to the place of the dead—what the Old Testament calls "Sheol"—then set free the righteous dead so they might ascend to heaven and preached the gospel to all who had never heard it. The scriptural origin of this idea may be found in 1 Peter 3:18b-20; 4:6. There we read, "He was put to death in the flesh, but made alive in the spirit, in which also he went and made a proclamation to the spirits in prison, who in former times did not obey"; and "the gospel was proclaimed even to the dead." Scholars debate the meaning of these verses, but they may point us toward what Jesus was doing on that Saturday. He may have done in the realm of the dead what he sought to do in his earthly ministry: "to seek out and to save the lost" (Luke 19:10). This doctrine and these verses would point to the depth of the passion Jesus Christ has for reaching people who have been alienated from God.

Matthew, in his account of the Crucifixion, tells the curious story that when Jesus died, some who had been dead were raised to life "and appeared to many" (Matthew 27:50-53). This too might be a scriptural anchor for the idea that Jesus set free those in the realm of Sheol who were righteous. Some go further and suggest that by entering the underworld, ruled by Satan, Jesus faced Satan himself and defeated him, not destroying him, but demonstrating his power over him. Even Martin Luther, in his *Solid Declaration*, suggested the devil was conquered in this descent to the dead. "We believe simply," he wrote, "that the entire person, God and human being, descended to Hell after his burial, conquered the devil, destroyed the power of Hell, and took from the devil all his power."[1] Both of these ideas are captured in classical art showing the gates of hell broken and Jesus leading Adam and Eve and the righteous of the Old Testament out of the realm of the dead toward the gates of heaven.

What Jesus actually did in the spirit while his body lay in the tomb will remain a mystery; but for his followers left behind on Earth, the period between his death and resurrection was as dark a time as any ever known. Holy Saturday represents despair and utter hopelessness.

## The Third Day

The third day began at sunset on Saturday night, but it was not until morning that Mary Magdalene discovered the stone had been rolled away and the tomb was empty. The details differ in each Gospel, but all agree that this woman who had been set free by Jesus from demon possession or mental illness was first on the scene. Matthew, Mark, and Luke tell us she was accompanied by one or more other women; and they had come with scented oils to anoint Jesus' body.

The women were thunderstruck by what they saw: The stone had been rolled away from the mouth of the tomb. They ran to the tomb, afraid someone had taken Jesus' body to desecrate it and humiliate him further. The Gospels vary somewhat in their accounts of what happened next. According to Mark (16:5), "they

saw a young man, dressed in a white robe." Matthew (28:2) identifies him as "an angel [a Greek word meaning "messenger"] of
the Lord." Luke (24:4) says that "suddenly two men in dazzling
clothes stood beside them." John (20:12) also tells us there were
"two angels in white." "They said... 'Why are you weeping?'"
(John 20:15). "Why do you look for the living among the dead?
He is not here, but has risen" (Luke 24:5). With that, the women
ran off to find the disciples.

The Easter chronology varies slightly in the four Gospel
accounts; but one thing is clear: The idea that Jesus had
been raised from the dead was considered unbelievable. In Mark
(16:1-8), the women learned Jesus had been raised; but they were
filled with terror and were afraid to tell anyone. In Matthew
(28:16-17), even after the disciples saw him on the mountain in
Galilee, "some doubted." In Luke (24:8-11), Mary and the others
told the disciples Jesus had been raised; "but these words
seemed to them an idle tale, and they did not believe them."
According to Luke (24:12), Peter ran to the tomb; but, while
"amazed," it is not clear whether he understood what had happened. In John's account (20:2-9), Peter and John ran to the tomb;
but though "they saw the linen wrappings lying there," they still
did not understand. Then there is "doubting Thomas," who
missed the first resurrection appearance of Jesus to the disciples.
Thomas told them, "Unless I see the mark of the nails in his
hands, and put my finger in the mark of the nails and my hand in
his side, I will not believe" (John 20:25).

How grateful I am for the Gospels and their willingness to
record that even the disciples struggled with doubt when it came
to the Resurrection. If the men and women who were with Jesus
found it difficult to believe, how much more so for people who
live twenty centuries later and have not seen the empty tomb or
the living Christ with their own eyes.

As a pastor, I find Easter both the most powerful and the most challenging Sunday on which to preach each year. It is challenging precisely because the events we celebrate are difficult to believe. Several dimensions of the story leave modern hearers joining with Thomas, saying, "Unless I see . . . I will not believe." Some interpreters have sought to make it easier to believe the Easter story. They have suggested alternatives to what the Gospels record. Perhaps Jesus was not really dead, and he was resuscitated. Perhaps he was dead, and the tomb was not really empty; the women and the disciples merely shared in a vision precipitated by wishful thinking. But the early church boldly asserted that the tomb was empty, that Jesus was bodily risen, and that he appeared to the apostles and to hundreds of others over a period of forty days. They saw him and talked with him. They touched his hands and assured themselves he really was alive. He was not a ghost. He was there with them. He even ate a meal with them. He taught and encouraged them. Thus Matthew ends his Gospel with these words Jesus spoke to his disciples: "This is what I want you to do," he told them. "I want you to preach the good news of the kingdom of God. I want you to make disciples of all people. Teach them what I taught you. Baptize them." And then he said, "And lo, even though you may not see me, you need to know this: No matter where you go, no matter what you do, until this age is over, I will be with you always" (paraphrase of Matthew 28:19-20).

There are many things in this world I do not fully understand and many which seem utterly absurd to me. Much of the realm of physics fits into this category. Did everything in the universe really come from an initial mass the size of the head of a pin? I do not see how that is possible, but current theories of the origin of the universe suggest this is so. Is my body really made up of atoms, each of which includes a nucleus surrounded by an electron cloud with constantly moving charged particles? I do not fully understand this, but I trust it is so. There are a host of other ideas

I have studied in physics that are so mind-boggling I cannot even describe them! So I ask myself, "Is it possible for the God who created the universe, who formed the atom, who wrote the DNA software that forms all living things, to reanimate, or transform and resurrect, the physical body of Jesus after his death?" Asked this way, the Resurrection does not seem so incredible.

Along with the question of the resurrection of Jesus' earthly body lies the larger question of whether there is life after death at all. The two are intertwined. If Jesus was raised from the dead, there is evidence for the reality of life after death; and if there is life after death, then Jesus' own resurrection would not seem difficult to believe.

There is no doubt the disciples were transformed following the Resurrection. These people who had deserted Jesus because they were afraid, who hid behind locked doors rather than help bury him, were now in the streets of Jerusalem proclaiming him to everyone. "Do with us what you want," they said. "Kill us if you must, but we have to tell you: The one you crucified we have seen raised from the dead. He is in fact the Son of God. He is the King of glory, the Savior of the world." They went from there throughout the world proclaiming the good news. They faced difficult times. They were arrested again and again, beaten, abused, and thrown into prison. Tradition has it that all but one of them were put to death for their faith, but they would never again dwell in those dark places of the spirit. No more would they feel the doubt and despair they felt before they had seen their risen Lord. They faced life with hope and confidence. When we hear, trust, and celebrate this Easter story, we reclaim the same faith and discover the same joy and hope the first disciples had. Easter has the power to change us.

## The Hope of Life After Death

The personal experience of many very different people leads me to conclude that there is life after death. I will recount just a few of more than fifty experiences shared with me over the years.

I sat with a man who was dying. Seated in his wheelchair, he asked if I could see "them," referring to people he could see that I could not. Not long afterward, he passed away. A woman dying in her nursing home bed, with her daughters by her side, said, "Can you hear them?" Her daughters told her they did not hear anything. "You can't hear them?" she said. "They are calling my name." They asked, "Who, Mom?" She named her deceased husband, her parents, and others who had passed on. Another woman told me recently of being awakened in the night. She looked up from her bed only to see her deceased husband, who had passed away several months before. There was a light shining on him; and he smiled at her, then vanished as she sat up in bed, wide awake.

Some time ago, I was sharing Don Piper's book *90 Minutes in Heaven* with a group of pastors. Piper was declared dead, had an experience of the afterlife, and then was brought back to life. A pastor came to me afterward and said, "My experience was very much like Piper's." He told me that he had been in a coma and that the prospects of his coming out of it were so dim his family decided to remove his life support. He told me he could hear his family members' tearful goodbyes. At that moment, an old friend who had died years before called his name. The friend told him not to worry, that he would be OK. The pastor felt a great peace come over him and felt a desire to follow his friend. He told me that what stood out to him was the sound of singing and music that seemed to emanate from heaven. Shortly afterward he opened his eyes and was restored to life. He told me, "I will never forget the peace and assurance that what was on the other side of death was marvelous."

I could go on and on with stories like these. To me, the variety of these experiences points to something real; and if there is life after death, then the testimony of the disciples, the women, and others that they had seen Jesus raised from the dead seems quite plausible. The fact is, the disciples were radically changed, empowered, emboldened, and filled with hope as a result of their encounter with the resurrected Christ. The apostle Paul reports that over five hundred people saw Christ after the Resurrection (1 Corinthians 15:6). He himself had an encounter with the risen Christ (Acts 9:1-18), a vision that transformed Paul from an enemy of Christianity to its greatest proponent. To me, the leap of faith required to believe in the resurrection of Christ is small. I am content to leave how it happened, the specific details of the Resurrection, in the realm of mystery. But *that* he was raised I feel content to trust as fact.

The Resurrection is not simply about a dead man being restored to life. Its power lies in its meaning, and here the Resurrection seems to me to be the perfect and essential ending to the gospel story. The resurrection of Christ, like his crucifixion, is a word from God speaking a profound truth that changes everything. This story defined the very lives of the earliest disciples. The apostle Paul summarized the role of the Resurrection in the gospel message in this way: "If you confess with your lips that Jesus is Lord and believe in your heart that God raised him from the dead, you will be saved" (Romans 10:9).

That leads to the last of the theories of the Atonement we will consider in this book. It is often referred to as "Christus Victor"—Christ the Victor. This view, popularized by Swedish theologian and bishop Gustaf Aulén, is said to be a restating of one of the dominant views of the Atonement held by the early church. It holds that the suffering, death, and resurrection of Christ must be taken together as a powerful word from God announcing God's victory over the powers of evil and over the sin that alienates us from God. They are God's triumph over death, which we, by faith, share.

I do not know that Aulén used this metaphor, but I find it helpful: In Jesus Christ, God entered a boxing arena to take on a very powerful enemy. This enemy, like the Philistine giant Goliath of old, held humanity captive. Human beings live in a world where "might is right" and where evil seems so often the victor. Even the "righteous" of Jesus' day were shown in the story of Christ's betrayal, condemnation, and death to be jealous, petty slaves to their own sin; and all of us are prisoners of the forces of death.

The reality of our enslavement to evil, sin, and death is evident all around us. It is seen in the 30,000 children who die each day of hunger and diseases related to malnutrition while others have plenty. It is seen in the continued wars and violent conflicts across the globe. It is seen in the selfishness and greed that have led to economic catastrophes, and it is seen in the pain we bring upon one another in our interpersonal relationships.

In Jesus, God entered the boxing arena where evil seems to have the upper hand. He took the worst blows of the enemy, being subject to the powers that conspired to destroy him. He was beaten, abused, and eventually knocked out. But just when the match seemed lost, Jesus arose; and in his resurrection he dealt a finishing blow to the forces of evil, sin, and death. Christ became the Victor. With his victory all humankind was offered the opportunity to join forces with him; to be set free from the power of evil, sin, and death; and to live lives of hope, freedom, and love.

Human beings still must choose to side with him. They are not forced to leave their enslavement to sin and death. The battle between good and evil will continue until Christ's return, but his death and resurrection dealt a decisive blow to the forces of evil and demonstrated the ultimate victory of God over it.

John's account of the Resurrection is the richest in symbolism, and he includes a host of clues pointing to the meaning of the victory Christ wrought through his death and resurrection.

Only John tells us Jesus' tomb was in a garden. We are meant to recall that the entire biblical narrative begins in a garden: the garden of Eden. There the devil tempted Adam and Eve to disobey God and pursue self-deification, bringing evil into the world. Humanity has been enslaved by self-interest and disobedience as well as by guilt and shame ever since. But in the garden where Jesus' tomb was located we see a reversal of Eden, giving those who choose to follow the crucified and risen Christ the chance to share in its restoration. They will work and pray for God's kingdom to come "on earth as it is in heaven."

John mentions that Mary Magdalene found two angels *inside* the tomb, sitting where the body of Jesus had been, one at the head and one at the feet. We are meant to envision in this scene the mercy seat of God, the symbolic throne that was the lid of the ark of the covenant. This is where the high priest offered the blood of atonement and made sin offerings before God. It reminds us that Christ has conquered death and administers mercy to all who call upon him.

## Vindication

Christ's resurrection is a vindication of his message, his identity, and his death on the cross. In his message, Jesus taught a way of life based upon the love of God and neighbor. He ministered to lost and broken people. One of the things that upset the religious authorities was that Jesus sat down with drunkards and prostitutes; he let them be part of his ministry. He taught that God was like a father who had two sons, one of whom ran away. The father was always waiting for that son to come back home again; he never stopped loving the runaway. That was the approach Jesus embodied in his ministry. His message about what God was like was completely countercultural. Blessed are the poor, the hungry, the meek, the lowly, the peacemakers. Blessed are you when you are persecuted for my name's sake.

When a Roman soldier beats you on the face, turn the other cheek and let him beat that one as well. When he demands that you carry his pack for a mile, carry it a second mile. Love not only your neighbors but also your enemies. Pray for those who persecute you. Don't forgive them just seven times, but seventy times seven. These were bizarre statements. How could anybody really live that way? But what he taught was vindicated by his resurrection.

The claims Jesus made about his own identity seemed just as bizarre. He said, "I am the bread of life. Whoever comes to me will never be hungry, and whoever believes in me will never be thirsty" (John 6:35). "I am the resurrection and the life. Those who believe in me, even though they die, will live" (John 11:25). "I am the way, and the truth, and the life. No one comes to the father except through me" (John 14:6). He repeatedly reinterpreted the traditions and teachings of the Jewish people, saying, "You have heard that it was said to those of ancient times.... But I say to you..." (Matthew 5:21-22). He said, "Go therefore and make disciples of all nations...teaching them to obey everything that I have commanded you" (Matthew 28:19-20). He claimed to be the Messiah, the Son of the living God. It was an idea the religious authorities and those awaiting a military messiah clearly rejected, but he claimed it yet again when questioned at his trial. All his claims were vindicated with his resurrection, something Paul notes in Romans 1:4 when he writes that Jesus "was declared to be the Son of God with power according to the spirit of holiness by resurrection from the dead."

The Resurrection also confirmed the meaning of Jesus' death on the cross: that it fulfilled a divine purpose, bringing about the forgiveness of sins. Luke captures this idea in a statement Jesus made to the disciples after the Resurrection: "Thus it is written, that the Messiah is to suffer and to rise from the dead on the third day, and that repentance and forgiveness of sins is to be proclaimed in his name to all nations, beginning from Jerusalem. You are witnesses of these things" (Luke 24:46-48).

In all three areas—his message, his identity, and his death on the cross—Jesus' resurrection vindicated everything he said, everything he did, and everything he was and is.

Ultimately, the Resurrection is the dramatic sign of God's victory over all the forces that conspired against Jesus—not just the Sanhedrin and the Romans, but all the forces of evil in the world. The Resurrection is also God's sign of victory over death. It signals that sin, evil, and death will not have the final word, though they may appear for a time to have the upper hand. The Resurrection is a shout of victory over all these things, proof that goodness, justice, and life will ultimately prevail. Paul writes, "The sting of death is sin, and the power of sin is the law. But thanks be to God, who gives us the victory through our Lord Jesus Christ" (1 Corinthians 15:56-57).

Christus Victor says the suffering, death, and resurrection of Jesus are God's response to the sin, evil, injustice, tragedy, and pain in this world. Jesus experienced all these things, and he triumphed over them. He invites all who choose to follow him to live as God's people, free from the power of sin and the fear of death. The power of Easter, and with it the Christus Victor theory of the Atonement, can be summarized in one word: *hope.* Hope is the sense that things will work out, that despite difficult circumstances and painful situations that might lead to despair, something good is around the bend. It is something we cannot live without. Dr. Jerome Groopman, who holds a chair in medicine at Harvard, notes in his book *The Anatomy of Hope,* "Hope gives us the courage to confront our circumstances and the capacity to surmount them. For all my patients, hope, true hope, has proved as important as any medication I might prescribe or any procedure I might perform."[2] This is what the story of Jesus' suffering, death, and resurrection brings to us.

Much of what is happening in our world is frightening. Several years ago *Time* magazine had a cover story about global warming that carried this headline: "Be Worried. Be Very Worried!" I believe global warming is a real threat and that Christians should be at the forefront of environmental stewardship, but I will not ultimately live my life in fear of it. Why? Because I believe that Christ is the Victor and that global warming will not have the final word in life.

The continuing threat of terrorism is very real. I believe we must find ways to address the underlying issues that create an environment for terrorists to flourish, but I will not live in fear of terrorism because Christ is the Victor and I do not believe terrorism will ultimately have the final word.

In 2008, a global economic crisis struck our world, one that will require fundamental changes in our relationship with money and affect nearly everybody in one way or another. Still, not even a global economic crisis can negate the fact that Christ is the Victor.

Knowing that Jesus will have the final word gives us courage when we face the problems of our time. That knowledge does not call us to hide in a room. It does not lead us to bury our heads and say we do not care about the problems we face. Of course we care about what is happening in our world, and because of the Resurrection we are able to face those things with hope and great courage.

Words attributed to Frederick Buechner capture it well: "Resurrection means the worst thing is never the last thing."

Over the years, I have cared for and loved many people in my congregation as they approached death. One remarkable man expressed the sense of the victory of Christ as well as anyone I have known. After years of trying to have children, he and his wife finally brought a little girl into this world. Then, months later, he was diagnosed with a rare and aggressive form of cancer. I sat by his bedside as the illness took over his body. He exhibited a remarkable faith in the midst of it. He said, "I know God doesn't give his children cancer. This is simply part of life. Of course I am praying to be made well. That is my desire. But even more than my own healing, I am praying that somehow, in the midst of my battle with cancer, the glory of God might be revealed in my life." He went on to say, "I know that Christ has risen; and because he lives, I will live. I know he has prepared a place for me. I am not afraid. And I trust that he will send people to care for my wife and my daughter. Like Paul, if I live longer, I will be grateful for that and hope to be useful to him. But if the cancer runs its natural course, I know I will be with him; and I am grateful for that. For to me, 'To live is Christ and to die is gain.' "

I have served as the senior pastor of the United Methodist Church of the Resurrection for almost twenty years as of this writing. I was twenty-five when my wife, my daughters, and I founded the church. Every Easter for twenty years I have ended my Easter sermon with the same words: "People ask me, 'Do you really believe this story of the Resurrection?' And my answer is always the same. I not only believe it, *I am counting on it.*"

I end this book with the words of Isaac Watts. They are from a hymn focused on the cross, and I believe they capture best the response God desires from us as we consider the events of the last twenty-four hours of Jesus' life:

> When I survey the wondrous cross
>   on which the Prince of Glory died,
> my richest gain I count but loss,
>   and pour contempt on all my pride.
>
> Forbid it, Lord, that I should boast,
>   save in the death of Christ my God;
> all the vain things that charm me most,
>   I sacrifice them to his blood.

See from his head, his hands, his feet,
   sorrow and love flow mingled down.
Did e'er such love and sorrow meet,
   or thorns compose so rich a crown?

Were the whole realm of nature mine,
   that were a present far too small;
love so amazing, so divine,
   demands my soul, my life, my all.[3]

Amen and Amen.

---

[1] From Harrowing of Hell; see http://en.wikipedia.org/wiki/Harrowing_of_Hell. (May 2008

[2] From *The Anatomy of Hope*, by Jerome Groopman, MD (Random House, 2004); page xiv.

[3] From "When I Survey the Wondrous Cross," in *The United Methodist Hynnal* (Copyright © 1989 by The United Methodist Publishing House); 298.

CPSIA information can be obtained at www.ICGtesting.com
Printed in the USA
LVOW121203090212

267912LV00001B/4/P